Ronald Jasper:

His Life, His Work and the ASB

RONALD JASPER

HIS LIFE, HIS WORK

AND THE ASB

DONALD GRAY

First published in Great Britain 1997
Society for Promoting Christian Knowledge
Holy Trinity Church
Marylebone Road
London NW1 4DU

British Library Cataloguing-in-Publication Data
A catalogue record of this book is available from
the British Library

ISBN 0-281-04976-9

Typeset by David Gregson Associates, Beccles, Suffolk
Printed in Great Britain by Biddles Ltd, Guildford and King's Lynn

CONTENTS

Preface

It may be thought strange to commence the acknowledgements and thanks in a biography with an expression of debt to the subject of the book. The fact is that the task of tackling this particular piece of work was made infinitely easier, because Ronald Jasper saved and then carefully ordered all his correspondence, memoranda and other significant documents.

On second thoughts, perhaps I should not to be too enthusiastically grateful! The result of all this careful filing was seventy boxes of material. Such a huge amount of documentation presents a biographer with both a challenge and a problem. The challenge is that it all needs to be read, the problem is that it calls for an immense amount of sifting and sorting, with the resulting worry, 'Have I got the balance right?' There was also another difficulty to be surmounted. Ronald Jasper's penultimate book, *The Development of Anglican Liturgy 1662–1980* contained a good deal of autobiographical material. While that is of great value to the biographer, it also means that the story of the most important and significant part of his life has recently been told. I have tackled this problem not by diminishing the importance of his work for the Liturgical Commission and the production of The Alternative Service Book, but by attempting to set it in a wider, and I trust more personal, context.

This does not mean I have ignored those autobiographical sections; in fact I have included a number of quotations from them. Additionally, a significant amount of the material that I have used to illustrate the last twenty years of his life has been derived from his correspondence. Indeed the book might have been entitled 'The Life and Letters of Ronald Jasper'.

My thanks must be expressed to the Jasper family, especially Mrs Betty Jasper. She not only allowed access to the material still housed in their retirement house at Ripon, but provided me with warm hospitality on my visits there. Ronald's literary executor is his son, the Revd Dr David Jasper. I wish to express my appreciation of all his enthusiastic help and assistance, not least the physical assistance which was needed in order to transport seventy boxes of papers to Westminster. All quotations from books, articles and letters of Ronald Jasper are made with Dr David Jasper's kind permission. All Ronald Jasper's papers including all his correspondence are now deposited in Lambeth Palace Library and will be catalogued by the staff. For this reason no detailed references have been given for this material.

The high affection in which Ronald was held is witnessed to by the large number of letters of reminiscences that I received from many of his colleagues and friends. I am grateful for the trouble they have taken in writing to me.

I acknowledge with thanks the help I received in acquiring details of various parts of Ronald Jasper's life. Plymouth College: the Revd Philip Arnold, R. M. Prideaux, John Spear. Leeds University: C. D. W. Sheppard (university library). Mirfield: Canon Dr G. R. Dunstan, the Revd J. H. Laxton, the Revd J. F. E. Morton, Fr Barry Orford CR, the Revd F. Wain, Canon Dr Alan Wilkinson. Ryhope: the Revd G. W. Fletcher, Canon David Goodacre, Mrs B. M. Young. St Oswald's Durham: the Revd Ben de la Mare. Esh and Langley Park: Miss Enid Eccleston, the Revd Gillian Pocock, Miss Ella Wright. St Giles Durham: Mrs Ellen Hutchinson, Miss Dorothy Meade. Durham University: Fr Alan Grainge SSJE, the Revd Ivor Scott-Oldfield, Dr C. D. Watkinson and Roger Norris (university library). Stillington: the Revd Malcolm Goodall. Exeter: the Very Revd Richard Eyre, Miss Angela Doughty (cathedral archives), Canon Dr J. A. Thurmer. King's College London: the Revd J. R. I. Wikeley. Southwark Ordination Course: the Revd H. C. Theobald. Westminster Abbey: the Revd Dr Edward Carpenter, the Abbey library and muniments room. York: C. B. L. Barr, Dr Charles Brown, James Fairbairn, the Rt Revd Lord Habgood, Canon Raymond Hockley, Canon John Toy, Dr John Shannon, Irvine Watson. Ripon: Canon Ronald McFadden, the Revd S. C. Jones, Dr David Smith. Liturgical Commission: Canon David Bishop, Bishop Cyril Bowles, Robin Brookes, the Revd Dr Paul Bradshaw, the Rt Revd Lord Coggan, Dr Lionel Dakers, Miss Daphne Fraser, Canon Douglas Vicary.

Others who supplied information include the Revd Dr Edgar Brown of the USA, John Edney of Dulwich, W. Hurworth (the Durham diocesan secretary), the Revd Dr Gordon Jeanes of St Michael's Llandaff, Paul Laxton of Liverpool University and Sister Perpetua OSB of West Malling Abbey. The libraries at the House of Commons, Lambeth Palace and Sion College all lived up to their well-deserved reputations for efficiency and helpfulness. My secretary Pamela Carrington undertook the sorting out of the necessary permissions to print quotations and helped with proofreading.

I owe particular thanks to Bishop Colin Buchanan, the Revd Raymond George and the Revd Jean and Canon Ralph Mayland who most kindly read and commented on particular chapters. Stephen Heard, however, gave generously of his time to read the whole manuscript and smoothed out many infelicities. The responsibility for the resulting text is, of course, my own.

The imperfections would have been even more numerous if my wife Joyce had not been the careful transposer of my autograph on to the newly-acquired word processor. My gratitude to her is enormous and we are both grateful for the skill with which the Revd Trevor F. Critchlow subsequently prepared the text for submission to the publishers.

The index has been compiled with the assistance of my daughter Alison Gray.

1 Little Cloister,
Westminster Abbey

ACKNOWLEDGEMENTS

I am grateful for permission to make quotations in the text from the following: Christopher Cocksworth, *Evangelical eucharistic thought in the Church of England*, 1993, Cambridge University Press; Edward Carpenter, *Archbishop Fisher: His Life and Times*, 1991, by permission of Canterbury Press Norwich; Richard Hughes, *Liturgical Language Today*, The Board of Mission, Church in Wales; Extract by Ronald Jasper in *Church Times*, 28 March 1958; Peter Hebblethwaite, *Paul VI, The First Modern Pope*, 1993, HarperCollins Publishers; Annibale Bugnini, *The Reform of the Liturgy 1948–1975*, 1975, The Liturgical Press; Paul A. Welsby, *A History of the Church of England 1945–1980*, 1984, by permission of Oxford University Press; Alan Wilkinson, *The Community of Resurrection: A Centenary History*, 1992, SCM Press Limited; Roger Lloyd, *The Church of England 1900–1965*, 1966, SCM Press Limited; Paul Bradshaw and Bryan Spinks, *Liturgy in Dialogue: Essays in Memory of Ronald Jasper*, 1993, used by permission of SPCK. Bishop Patrick Rodger has allowed me to use the verse on page 111 and Dr David Frost kindly gave his consent to the inclusion of the extract from *Anti-Memo I* on pages 116–17.

1

Boyhood, University and Mirfield

The fact that the main architect of the greatest changes in the worship of the Church of England for three hundred years should have been born and brought up in the far south-west of England might be surprising. Yet it ensured that he would always be a real representative of the man and woman in the pew. He was not a son of the vicarage, like so many clergy were even until recent times, nor was he the product of the cloistered calm of our foremost public schools, or Oxbridge. He may at times have been slightly embarrassed by his redbrick university education, but he had that in common with the majority of those who won through from a similar background to that level of higher education. Leadership in the Church of England should not be the preserve of any class, certainly not of any particular school, university or theological college, and Ronald Jasper's massive influence on church affairs can be justified not only by his academic skills but also because he represented in himself the real parochial and pastoral roots of the church.

His parents do not seem to have had any particular connection with the church. They were not as we say, 'church people'. Ronald was not given any particular lead by his parents in this regard. He was baptized on 11 October 1917 at St Mark's Ford, Devonport by the curate of the parish, the Revd V. Dorman Harris, but there are no early Sunday school prizes among his possessions and the first sign of any religious activity does not come until he is at Plymouth College.

Early years

Ronald Claud Dudley Jasper was born on 17 August 1917, at 4 York Terrace, Ford, Devonport, arriving in the last year of the First World War. His father, from whom he inherited the Christian name

'Claud', which was later to fascinate his fellow students at Mirfield, worked in the dockyard. His mother was Florence Lily. The Jaspers had been married just over twelve years when Ronald was born.

Ronald's father, Claud Albert Jasper, had left school just before his fifteenth birthday in July 1897 and followed his own father, Samson, into the dockyard. Claud was apprenticed to Willoughby Brothers Shipbuilders, of Devonport. He completed his apprenticeship in 1904, twelve months before his wedding to Florence Curtis. Samson Jasper was a much respected sawyer, a particularly skilled dockyard occupation concerned with preparing wood for shipbuilding. He received the Imperial Service Order in 1905 'for meritorious service in Devonport Dockyard'. It was to the next grade of skilled dockyard craftsmen that his son Claud belonged – he became a shipwright, whereas Ronald's maternal grandfather, Samuel Curtis, belonged to the grade below, that of skilled labourer. To be a shipwright, in the words of a correspondent who has studied the economic life of Plymouth during that period, was to be 'an aristocrat of the skilled working classes'. It was thought to be security of employment for life.

At that point in the war, Claud Jasper and his fellow workmen in the dockyard were working long and hard hours both building and repairing the ships that were so very necessary for 'the war effort'. It would also have been a time of relative affluence and afforded the Jaspers the opportunity of accumulating savings. These would not have been large, but a skilled craftsman could expect to live modestly and comfortably, bringing up his children with an expectation that they, in their day, might aspire to even better circumstances. In the event the Jaspers had no further children so that they were able to concentrate their aspirations on Ronald. Is it fanciful to detect in their decision to give him three Christian names that even at the time of his baptism they were dreaming of their son's future?

Claud Jasper left a small notebook in which he had carefully noted the most important events in his life. After detailing his dockyard apprenticeship, his marriage and the birth of his son, he believed two other occasions were worthy of an entry. As both occurred during Ronald's childhood, it would be surprising if he was not caught up in the excitement.

In 1926 Claud went with a group of friends to Wembley for the FA cup final and saw Bolton Wanderers beat Manchester City by one goal to nil. This was no quick trip: they stayed on in London until the following Saturday and took in Paul Whiteman's band at the Tivoli, *Rose Marie* at Drury Lane and *The Farmer's Wife* at the Royal Court. As we shall discover, the theatre and particularly the musical theatre, was a continuing interest of Ronald's, so we can reasonably speculate that Claud's account of his week in London did not fall on deaf ears as far as his son was concerned.

The second experience, or more accurately group of experiences, concerned his working life. In 1930 Claud Jasper spent a fortnight at sea on board HMS *Glorious* during her sea trials. Then just after the outbreak of war in 1939 he took part in the sea trials of HMS *Valiant*. These experiences would also have provided many tales to tell a growing lad. They would also have provided welcome ammunition for Florence Jasper's campaign to persuade her son to join the Royal Navy. It did not succeed, and Ronald came no nearer than being a twelve-year-old midshipman in an amateur production of *HMS Pinafore* at the Repertoire Theatre in Plymouth.

Ronald Jasper's earliest education was received at Ford primary school in Plymouth. In Plymouth, as in other towns and cities of a similar size, the ambition of parents was for their sons to win through to a grammar school education. They realized it was a narrow gate. The more well-off and affluent were able to provide this type of education for their child by enrolling him as a fee-paying scholar. True, there was a basic examination to pass so that standards were maintained, but the element of competition was absent and the decision was mostly parental – could or would they afford it? For the Jaspers the affluent wartime days were over, and in 1928 the only possible route to the prized grammar school education was via the scholarship system.

Plymouth College

Plymouth College (or to give it its full name at that time 'Plymouth and Mannamead College') was founded in 1877 by a group of local worthies including Bishop Frederick Temple, then Bishop of Exeter, two local non-conformist ministers and the vicar of St Andrew's Plymouth (Prebendary G. T. Wilkinson). It was a non-sectarian school, but with a firmly Christian basis. The school's historian tells how it was intended that the school should serve Plymouth and the district much as Bristol Grammar School serves Bristol, 'but with ambitions similar to those of another Bristol foundation, Clifton

College. Clifton had been in fact a main source of inspiration and an exemplar to our own founders.'[1]

Claud and Florence Jasper must have been delighted at the news of Ronald's success in the scholarship examination and proud of him as he entered form 2a of Plymouth College in September 1928, joining some boys who had come through the preparatory school. He arrived, as one of the former 'prep' boys Jack Woolley recalled, 'quiet, studious and smiling. Fresh-faced, fair-haired and upright; upright physically and in a moral way but nevertheless cheerful. He was "different" from most of us who had come through the more expensive route of the college's own preparatory school, for one thing he was brighter.'

Another contemporary writes, 'Nearly half the intake into form 2a each year were boys who had "won a scholarship" by passing high on the eleven-plus from their elementary school. I think, but cannot be sure, that Jasper was one of these. This intake produced some of the cleverest boys in the school, and the most hard-working. There was no snobbery among the pupils about our method of entry, and not much (visible) among the staff.'

So commenced in earnest a life of study and research, which continued until the very last weeks of his life. However, it cannot be suggested that in those early years at the college he showed more than the average ability expected of a scholarship boy. On leaving the third form he, like everyone else, was given the option of taking German or Greek. He chose German. A contemporary, John Spear, who was with him at school, suggests that the choice is evidence that Ronald had no thought at all at the time of being ordained. Two years later in July 1932 he took the Oxford and Cambridge School Certificate in which he gained five credits (English, history, French, German and mathematics). He passed in scripture and Latin. This was reckoned as a good, but not brilliant, performance. Half a dozen others taking the examination at the same time did better. Yet it gave him the desired 'matric' exemption; the necessary qualification to proceed further with his studies.

Now came the necessity of choosing his subjects of study more narrowly. In the end, and no doubt on advice, he wisely decided upon three of the subjects in which he had gained credits at school certificate level: French, German and history. The usual pattern was to spend three years in the sixth form – indeed four years was not unknown in those days.

From his first term in the modern sixth until he left the college, Ronald preserved the termly reports sent to his parents by the headmaster H. W. Ralph. To begin with they are evidence of worthy but unspectacular academic achievement. For instance his English master finds that his idiom is a little unnatural at times and believes he ought to read more widely. This advice seems to have been heeded, because twelve months later the same master believes that Ronald's essays 'show a distinct improvement in style'. It is a similar story in German: by 1933 his work is more reliable and his French shows definite progress. In the class lists his name appears at a midpoint.

But is it fair to delve more deeply into these judgements of his schoolmasters? How many of us would want to be judged on our performance at that stage of life? Sufficient to say that even then a pattern was being established – Ronald Jasper would always work long, hard, and carefully to achieve results that were accurate and reliable.

During his second year in the sixth he improved his School Certificate mark in Latin by obtaining a credit, but his interests were moving more and more towards history rather than languages. Ronald worked towards the European history examination, and about this time he decided that he would aim for reading history at university.

Discovering the Church

In a biography such as this we want to discover the first awakening of interest in religious matters. This is not easy. Ronald Jasper never wrote any biographical notes about this period of his life, or about the burgeoning of his Christian faith. The only notes (and then they are very brief indeed) cover a period nearly twenty years later. So we can only speculate, basing our speculations on what evidence we have. Jasper the historian would approve, I am sure.

Music was always important to Ronald and as a boy he attained a modicum of proficiency on the piano. In the Associated Boards 'school' (lower division) examination he obtained a pass with honourable mention in the pianoforte in 1929. In November of that same year he took part in a competition entitled 'Festival of British Music' held in Plymouth, and organized by the British Music Society. In the section for piano solo for boys under fourteen, he obtained 85 per cent and gained a first class grading. This piano-playing skill was later displayed at Plymouth College. There are a number of mentions of his piano playing in the school magazine. For example: 'Jasper provided sweet music at our annual display of Thespian Pyrotechnics.' By the age of fifteen he was playing regularly for the school's morning prayers. In fact the headmaster regularly expressed his appreciation: 'He has been of very great assistance musically,' is a typical remark.

So his first recorded 'religious' activity was playing the hymns at school assembly, but this does not connect him with the Church. To find the first evidence of this we have to rely on the memory of schoolmate John Spear. He recalls that Ronald had become involved with St Bartholomew's church and had persuaded John to help him in the running of the Scouts, which he did for a year.

St Bartholomew's was one of the churches in the parish of Stoke Damerel, and among Ronald's personal papers is one of the few things that he kept from those Plymouth days, an undated cutting from the parish magazine:

> I feel you will all wish to join me in wishing God speed to one of the younger members of our Church who is about to embark upon his training for Holy Orders.
>
> Ronald C. Jasper has been known to many of us at the Church as head server and an energetic worker in Sunday School and choir. He is now shortly to depart for the training college at Mirfield, Yorkshire, and I feel sure that the prayers and good wishes of the congregation will go with him. It is not often that a Church as young as ours has the privilege of submitting a candidate for Holy Orders. *L. B. McCarthy.*

Legh Beauchamp McCarthy was ordained in 1933 to serve as a curate at the parish of Stoke Damerel. After Oxford he had been at Wells Theological College, a High-Church college, and was serving under the rector of the parish, Prebendary Thomas Collins Walters who was also the Rural Dean. The tradition of the parish was Anglo-Catholic.

How and when Ronald discovered his vocation to the priesthood we cannot say. This was a personal matter, the details of which he never shared with his family. It was something very precious to him, a calling which he seems never to have doubted. In all his work he was always priestly without ever being pompous or parsonic. He left school with the avowed intention of training for Holy Orders, his choice of university was part of that. There is no mention of this decision, even in passing, on his final school report, but the school magazine (April 1935), in the 'Thompson's House Notes', congratulates him on obtaining a place at the College of the Resurrection, Mirfield – unusually with no mention of Leeds University.

At school he was an enthusiastic member of two societies. He could not have imagined, for example, that his membership of the Literary and Debating Society would be a preparation for innumerable sermons, lectures and addresses to come, to say nothing of the debates of the Convocation, the Church Assembly and eventually the General Synod. Roy Prideaux who was also at school with Ronald writes to say:

> My copies of the *Plymothian*, the school magazine which I was editing during my last year, show that on Friday, Feb. 2nd 1934, he read a paper on 'A South American Cruise', giving an interesting description of the expedition made by the Prince of Wales to Brazil and incidents *en route*. In March he had the temerity to enter for the Debating Challenge Cup, receiving 26 votes to the runner-up's 168, and my 222! This suggests that he may have won it the following year (when other contestants had moved on to Oxford).

He was certainly very keen on debating; seconding a motion that 'mankind must throw off the bondage of the machine or perish' in December 1932 and proposing that 'Germany is destined to cause the destruction of Europe' the following year.

His second interest, and one that he took with him into his parochial ministry, was drama. The school magazine records that in 1934 he acted in two one-act plays: *Birds of a Feather*, and the well-known and often performed *The Monkey's Paw*. A kindly review said: 'R. C. D. Jasper gave perhaps his best performance so far as Mr Martock. His embarrassment and restraint portrayed vividly the difficulty of his position, and was another contribution to the natural atmosphere in which the very unnatural events took place.'

Young Ronald had also trodden the boards on earlier occasions at his school. Carefully tucked away among his personal mementoes is the programme for the Literary and Debating Society's annual entertainment in March 1931. In Lord Dunsany's *A Night at the Inn*, thirteen-year-old R. C. D. Jasper is listed as playing one of the priests. An early omen? In April 1933 in a concert in aid of the Mayor of Plymouth's 'Christmas Cheer' Fund, the *Plymothian* records that 'In *The Master of the House* R. C. Jasper made the most convincing girl we have seen on stage for a long time: perhaps it was the same wig that worked another miracle upon an actor in the next play.'

His sporting activities at school were more limited. In rugby Ronald got no further than fourth XV colours (despite scoring two of the three tries against Sutton Secondary!) but he was a keen Fives player out of school, having a regular place in the North Town Fives team. He was still playing this game as a university chaplain in Durham fifteen years later. Ronald also joined the school Scout troop, contributing regularly to their annual entertainment. Towards the end of his time at Plymouth College he became a prefect, and also House Captain of Thompson's. These activities impressed the headmaster who described Ronald as 'an invaluable member of his form and the various school societies'. Upon his departure from Plymouth College the headmaster remarked, 'He has served the School well.'

As Fr McCarthy had revealed in the Parish Magazine, on leaving school the young Jasper had one objective – ordination. Roy Prideaux, who shared a year in the sixth form with Ronald was also at that time 'a devout Anglo-Catholic, a Sunday School teacher and about to go to Keble as a prospective ordinand'. But he admits, 'neither of us would have paraded our faith much in the school environment.'

Leeds University and the Hostel of the Resurrection

In October 1935 at the age of eighteen, Ronald moved to Leeds to commence a five-year course leading to ordination in the Church of England. He was the youngest of his year. Those who were believed by the Community of the Resurrection to be capable of a university education (apart from those who had already obtained a degree elsewhere), were housed in the Hostel of the Resurrection near the university.

The Community of the Resurrection, founded by Charles Gore in 1892, had commenced ordination training at Mirfield in 1903 by converting the stable block for this purpose. As Alan Wilkinson, the historian of the Community of the Resurrection, has recorded: 'An appeal was launched; the training would be free but students would be expected to provide their own clothes and pocket money. After ordination and before any engagement to marry, they would be asked to repay half the cost of training (i.e. usually £125) over five or six years.'[2]

A year later the Community took over two houses at Springfield Mount in Leeds to provide temporary accommodation so that ordinands might take degrees at what was then the Yorkshire College (but which in 1904 became Leeds University), before proceeding to the theological course at Mirfield. The college was officially affiliated to the university in 1904. In 1907 an appeal was launched for funds to provide a permanent hostel in Leeds, the first part of which was opened and blessed in 1910. Many of the early Mirfield students came from working-class and lower-middle-class backgrounds. So the young Ronald Jasper arrived at the Hostel of the Resurrection in Leeds, with its ordered life and worship, having only rarely spent any time away from his parents' home. The Revd J. F. E. Morton, a fellow student, recalls the lifestyle:

> It may help if I try to give some account of the Mirfield system of those days. For most, the initial stage was a quite imposing hall of residence (still standing) from which students went out to degree courses at Leeds University nearby. Parents were asked to make donations, if able. From Ronald's, none were forthcoming. Once accepted, every need, except clothes and vacations, was supplied – doctors and dentists, laundry, even pocket money. I can remember two separate cases of TB, who were sent to sanatoria, and maintained there until recovery. The supervision was benevolent, but firm. People were sent away for slackness and scholastic failures – although in some cases of the latter, a second chance was given. When we got to Mirfield, one or two additional students might join us from other Universities, but not many in those days. With such drop-outs and additions, the final year was not quite the same as the first. Ronald and I survived.

Ronald chose to study history at Leeds University, and found British constitutional history of particular fascination. At the end of his third year he obtained a second class degree, while two of his contemporaries, Harry Hare and Gordon Dunstan, obtained first class degrees in history.

No one was surprised that Gordon Dunstan should then be offered a bursary to study for an MA; the surprise was that Professor Hamilton Thompson should offer Ronald Jasper a similar opportunity for further study. The reason can be found in the work that Ronald put into his thesis which was part of the final examination. Professor Thompson recognized the potential in Ronald's work. He thought he detected the making of a good researcher: 'the thesis which he presented as part of the work required for his degree of BA was a production of distinct merit upon a subject which gave proof of his ability for original research.' Time proved the professor's hunch correct. However, Ronald did not take up the offer of the bursary and chose to proceed to the college at Mirfield and do the work for his higher degree alongside his theological studies. This was a risky undertaking, involving a good deal of extra work, not least in the vacations, but he eventually did it.

During his time at university, music once again provided Ronald with a respite from study. He joined the University Music Society, contributing to the tenor line in performances of such works as Haydn's *The Seasons*, Handel's *Acis and Galatea* and Stanford's *Six Elizabethan Pastorals*. Also carefully preserved amongst his souvenirs of undergraduate days are a particular series of press photographs, in which he features clearly. *The Yorkshire Post* and other papers carried pictures of the Hostel choir rehearsing for a programme of carols to be given both at the Hostel and in York Minster. As they sang in the Minster none of that small choir could have guessed that they had a future Dean of York in their midst. Ronald recalled it fifty years later: 'I was a member of a little group of eight students who did a kind of King's Singers act, although we never achieved the latter's fame or brilliance. We were invited to give a recital of music at York Minster just before Christmas: and after we had duly performed, the Dean took us off to a marvellous supper at Terry's – I can still remember it – fresh salmon and all that goes with it in that wonderful panelled dining room.'[3]

Mirfield

The period spent at Mirfield was intended not only for theological study and examination, but also for spiritual preparation. The college had its own chapel and worship, but was also part and parcel of a religious community, with an ordered round of devotions punctuating the day.

Just before Ronald took up residence at Mirfield, the great Community Church was completed and consecrated by Archbishop William Temple. It is likely that, having received his BA degree at the Congregation in Leeds on Monday 4 July, he and other members of the Hostel were present at the consecration on Thursday 7 July 1938. Charles Gore the founder had died in 1932, and the completed church was planned to contain Gore's tomb. In the event, by the day of consecration the church also contained the tomb of another of the Order's founding fathers. Bishop Walter Frere, having resigned his See of Truro and returned to Mirfield, was entrusted with the task of drafting a consecration service for the newly-built church. Unfortunately he did not live to see the day of the service and died on 2 April 1938. The tombs of Gore and Frere now flanked the high altar of the new church. So Ronald never had the opportunity of sitting at the feet of Frere, that great liturgical scholar, while he was at Mirfield. When later in 1953 he came to edit Frere's *Correspondence on Liturgical Revision and Construction*, he did not reveal whether or not he had ever met the man whose 'sincerity of purpose and saintliness' he paid tribute to in his introduction. Only later did he disclose that he had met Frere in his boyhood days in the diocese of Truro. In a *Church Times* article in 1958 Ronald was presumably drawing on personal memories when he wrote: 'The vision still remains of a bearded figure in a purple cassock, tall, slim, very upright, hands clasped behind the back, walking with that rather peculiar springing step, and losing nothing of dignity for being capped by a minute and battered trilby hat. Dignity – and also sanctity: for he was a man for whom worship was the very essence of life, the first of interests and the most normal of habits.'[4]

None the less, in those days there were many other notable CR Fathers from whom a young ordinand could gain inspiration. One in particular continued as a friend and counsellor of Ronald's for the next twenty-five years. This was Thomas Hannay. In the estimation of Alan Wilkinson, he was one of the two outstanding principals of the College of the Resurrection between the wars. The other was Timothy Rees. Interestingly, both he and Fr Hannay were persuaded to allow themselves to be elected Bishop outside the Church of England: Rees in Wales and Hannay in Scotland – where he subsequently became Primus.[5]

Historical research

The last exams before ordination were taken in the spring of 1940, while the 'phoney war' concluded and the grim storm clouds of war gathered. It was customary for Mirfield ordinands to be presented at the Michaelmas ordinations, but in the circumstances it was decided to bring them forward to Trinity. However, there was a snag in Ronald's case. By Trinity 1940 he had not attained the canonical age for being made deacon, which is twenty-three, so he had to wait until September and the Michaelmas ordinations. But as ordination exams were now over (he had been awarded a *bene* in church history), there was time to give a last-minute polish to the MA dissertation on which he had been working alongside his work for the ordination exams. For his honours degree he had specialized in modern history with particular reference to European diplomacy; for his Master's he had been researching the area of constitutional history, not under Professor Thompson, but with Professor A. S. Turberville.

Parliamentary representation was the focus of Ronald's work, and in particular the representative history of a rotten borough not far from his native heath. This was Grampound in Cornwall, disenfranchised in 1824 for corruption. As Professor Turberville wrote later, 'He showed himself to be a student of ability and of marked keenness and enthusiasm which he evinced more particularly in the thesis which he wrote for his Honours Degree and still more in the mature studies which he undertook for the degree of MA.' The dissertation which Ronald submitted was regarded by the examiners as worthy of a distinction. In his first few years after ordination he maintained this 'keenness and enthusiasm' for constitutional history, corresponding with Dr George Veitch, the distinguished Professor of History at Liverpool University.[6] Professor Veitch was very interested in the research Ronald was doing.

Ronald's first publication appeared in 1941 in the *Bulletin of the Institute of Historical Research*,[7] and comprised a series of corrections to the entry on Sir John Trevor (MP for Grampound in the Long Parliament), in the *Dictionary of National Biography*. Two years later he produced a more substantial piece of work in *The English Historical Review*,[8] entitled, 'Edward Eliot and the acquisition of Grampound'. Though an impressive start to what was to prove to be a lifetime of writing and research, there is no sign yet of liturgical research. In brief notes, partly typed and partly handwritten, that he left among his papers, he wrote:

> Both as a student and in my first curacy my interest in matters of worship was not great. My passion was Constitutional History. Before ordination I had already gained a research degree in that subject, being fortunate enough to secure the unusual and coveted award of a distinction. It was not surprising therefore that my teachers encouraged me to go further in this field and if possible seek a university appointment. Unfortunately the outbreak of the 1939–1945 war put paid to any ideas of this and I was ordained in Durham Cathedral in 1940.[9]

NOTES

1. Charles Robert Serpel, *Plymouth College: An Historical Sketch*, Plymouth, 1950, p. 5.
2. Alan Wilkinson, *The Community of the Resurrection: A Centenary History*, London, 1992, p. 279.
3. Ronald Jasper, *Herbert Newell Bate, 1871–1941: A Reticent Genius*, York, 1987, p. 1.
4. *Church Times*, 28 March 1958, p. 10, (see also Guy W. Hockley in C. S. Philips (ed.), *Walter Howard Frere*, 1947, pp. 76ff).
5. Edward Luscombe, *The Scottish Episcopal Church in the Twentieth Century*, Edinburgh, 1996, p. 157.
6. Thomas Kelly, *For Advancement of Learning: The University of Liverpool 1881–1981*, Liverpool, 1981, p. 199.
7. *Bulletin of the Institute of Historical Research*, 1941, vol. 18, no. 54, p. 136.
8. Ronald Jasper, 'Edward Eliot and the acquisition of Grampound', *The English Historical Review*, 1943, vol. 58, no. 232, pp. 475–81.
9. Ronald Jasper, 'My development as a Liturgist', (ed. David Jasper), *The Friends of York Minster 62nd Annual Report 1991*, p. 17.

2

PARISH LIFE AND THE BEGINNING OF LITURGICAL STUDY

RONALD WAS ORDAINED at Michaelmas 1940 in Durham Cathedral. In the same notes in which he details his early historical interests, Ronald says that it was the Principal at Mirfield, Fr Hannay, who suggested he work in the Durham diocese, partly for the proximity of the university, and partly for the Bishop, Dr A. T. P. Williams. Ronald commented: 'Dr Williams was himself a distinguished historian (he had been known at Winchester as "History Bill") and it was thought that as an academic he would be prepared to keep a benevolent eye on a young man with historical interests.'[1] This proved to be very true. Among the few personal letters that Ronald preserved, the letters from Fr Hannay only slightly outnumber those of Dr Williams. It is very evident that the latter did keep a benevolent eye on Ronald Jasper, following, encouraging and advising him as his career developed, and believing him to be one of his protégés.

Curate at Ryhope

A COAL-PIT VILLAGE

Ronald served his 'title' (his initial curacy) in a pit village called Ryhope near Sunderland, under the Vicar James Armstrong Little. Of Ryhope itself, the Revd G. W. (Robin) Fletcher who became Vicar in 1981 has written: 'It's a peculiarly self-contained community rather arrogant about itself – but recognises its failings. I was informed shortly after coming here that Ryhope was really "the Harrogate of the North". In a way, though, it has had quite a history.'

Ryhope's coal-pit opened in April 1856 and closed in November 1966. In recent times EC money has ensured that the scars have been removed – as indeed they have over just about all the Durham coalfield. Ryhope is now a desirable dormitory for Sunderland. It is built on a magnesian limestone slope that drops, over a mile, gradually from about 200 feet to the sea.

The parish contains a mental institution, Cherry Knowle. Vicar Fletcher writes:

> Although it is now much run down, when I came here 12 years ago there were at least 1000 patients there. I am told that when in full swing there were of the order of 1400. Not surprisingly, it was the biggest employer in Ryhope – after the Pit. The life of Cherry Knowle had a remarkable influence on the village itself. People were, and still are *most* tolerant. If a patient wandered down into the village with no clothes on, nobody batted an eyelid. Somebody (anybody) would simply wrap a blanket round him, push him into a car and drive him back up again!

Second, there is Ryhope General Hospital. In 1939 the hospital made ready to receive war wounded, and the first patients from the battlefield arrived at Ryhope in May 1940, round about the time of Dunkirk. The 'temporary' buildings are still there! At the time, nurses and ancillary staff were very much in demand. And so were the clergy.

Then there is the pit. Fletcher writes:

> I think I'm right in saying that it employed about 1600 men when at full throttle. There were similar pits all around the place: few of them were much more than two and a half miles from their neighbours, so there was a huge underground maze. In those days (the 1940s) I don't think they extended out to sea. Men were killed in pit accidents with pretty monotonous regularity. There were 119 recorded fatalities in the lifetime of the one here, but it's a lower number than some others since there were no big methane blow outs. Even so, that figure needs treating with some reserve: when a man was fatally injured, they moved heaven and earth to get him away from the pithead before he died. No prizes are offered for guessing why!
>
> Ryhope miners had a reputation for bloody-mindedness even greater than that in other pits round about – which I think is saying something. I have heard more than one old union man say that the reason for Ryhope's being the first local pit to close was almost certainly due to this.

English Protestant and Irish Roman Catholic immigrants came to this north-eastern area in the 1860's. The two communities were always separate, and to a certain extent antagonistic: intermarriage was definitely frowned upon. And there was real geographical segregation. One part of the parish, originally called Hollycarrside, was renamed Cardknuckles and Vinegar Hill after places in Ireland. These divisions were already breaking down before the pit closed; they are hardly noticeable now. But they were certainly strong in Ronald Jasper's time. Fletcher sums up Ryhope by saying, 'The community spirit here is still strong, even for an old Co. Durham village.'

RYHOPE CHURCH: PAST AND PRESENT

Ryhope's church was consecrated in 1874 and added to in 1932. Robin Fletcher writes of it as 'Nothing terribly special – seats about 400 comfortably. It replaced an earlier Chapel of Ease that had been built in 1840 and adjoined the village green. That chapel ceased to be used for public worship in 1874 and became the Church School. A new Church Junior School was built opposite the new Church in 1898, and the old Chapel of Ease continues as the Infant's Department.'

James Armstrong Little, Ronald Jasper's vicar, is said by the present vicar to be the architect of the Parish of Ryhope as we find it today. Little had succeeded a man called Percival Knight who remains a legend in Ryhope to this day. Knight regarded everything and everyone within the boundaries of his parish as belonging to his own personal fiefdom and there is little doubt that he was revered by all. He was incredibly energetic and could be a real tyrant. He remained a bachelor.

Knight was obviously a difficult man to follow, and Fletcher suspects that James Little always felt under his shadow. When he departed for Norham in 1946 he confided to one or two people that he felt Ryhope didn't really want him and he got a delightful shock when Ryhope people descended on him in droves afterwards.

For Fr Little, all parish policy was based on the Offices and the daily Eucharist. Sunday worship became: 8.00 a.m. Holy Communion, 11.00 a.m. sung Eucharist, 6.30 p.m. Evensong. Matins replaced the sung Eucharist every first Sunday in the month. Vestments were worn, but there was no incense or Reservation. Little, apparently, had a 'thing' about getting everyone into the confessional, and that did get a lot of backs up. Memories are of a deeply compassionate man – tall, a bit hunched, with a great beak of a nose. Unlike Percival Knight, he was married, and his wife, among other things, started the Mothers' Union: which even now is still one of the biggest branches in the Durham diocese.

Little's chief targets outside the church itself were the Hospitals and the Schools. There is little doubt that he and his curates taught there regularly. Fr Fletcher reports that girls who were at the school 'over the road' still speak about Ronald Jasper. Indeed he reports that 'heart throb' was the expression used!

The present incumbent also says that there is rather more to tell about the hospitals in the parish. As chaplain to the mental hospital, Little was up there every Sunday afternoon taking a service. Then in May 1940 the first casualities started to arrive at the newly-built general hospital. Sunday services were taken there too – on the wards because there was no chapel – and members of the congregation were cajoled into going to the hospital in order to hand out hymnbooks, sing, and generally befriend the patients. 'There were some rather nice young ladies involved in all this and I have heard of at least three romances that finished up at the altar!' writes Robin Fletcher.

Since the patients came from all over the United Kingdom, some provision had to be made for housing their families when they came to visit. The vicarage became the main 'hotel', and members of the congregation were persuaded to open up their homes too. St Paul's, Ryhope, had reason to be proud of itself in those days.

Up to about 1943, Sunderland was the object of a certain interest on the part of the *Luftwaffe* – especially the shipyards at Pallion, only three or four miles away. On the whole Ryhope got off lightly, getting only one stick of bombs that caused any damage, whereas back in the south-west of England Ronald's home town of Plymouth had suffered much worse. In March and April 1941 Hitler's *blitzkrieg* reached that part of England. On 2 April Ronald went down to Plymouth and took his mother back to Ryhope. It was as well that he did, because after raids on Devonport later that month, Ronald's father Claud in a brief 'Blitz Diary' which he kept, recorded 'House at 32 Furneaux Road uninhabitable'.

In the midst of all this, there was obviously a great deal of praying to be done by both priests and people. The church at Ryhope was always open, and short services were held to pray for and with people in trouble at almost any time of day or night.

Mrs B. M. Young of Ryhope recalls those days: 'Ronald Jasper was initiated into Mental Hospital and General Hospital visiting at the very beginning of his ministry in Ryhope.' Mrs Young gives more details. 'On a Thursday evening Evensong was sung, and on Sunday Holy Communion or Mattins, at the Mental Hospital, and on Sunday evenings there were short services in the Wards at the General Hospital, taken alternately by the Vicar and Ronald Jasper together with the Deaconess and a small group of people. In the winter time it was black dark and we used to walk to the hospital carrying torches covered with blue tissue paper to subdue the light. We always managed to get back to the church before the sermon was preached.'

During his ministry at Ryhope, Ronald Jasper formed a small mixed youth club which met in the vicarage on a Sunday night after church. He lived at the vicarage, having his own rooms. In the lounge was a lovely grand piano. Mrs Young recalls, 'On occasions he would invite those who were interested in music, and he, being a good pianist, and having a good singing voice, would play and sing to us West Country songs. Sometimes a friend, Lily Brandon, and I would play pianoforte duets.'

In 1942 the time came for Ronald Jasper to move on, but not before he had made the acquaintance of the domestic science mistress of the church school at Ryhope, Miss Betty Wiggins of Seaham Harbour.

Parochial life in Ryhope did not leave much time for historical research, although the bishop had put him in touch with both the history and the theology departments of Durham University. 'I spent what time I could working in the University Library,' he wrote. After two years the bishop moved him into the city of Durham itself, thus making the libraries and other facilities of the university easily available. Ronald was very appreciative of this kindness, which turned out to have far-reaching consequences.

Curate at St Oswald's Durham

The biographical notes Ronald was preparing just before his death, of which he completed less than a thousand words, are headed, 'My development as a Liturgist'. Thankfully, he was able to record for us the awakening of an interest in the history and development of liturgy. This began in the parish of St Oswald's Durham, to which the Bishop sent him. It was not a large parish and its congregation was eclectic. Ronald was not stretched by the parochial work: duties were light, he said, and gave him plenty of opportunity for study. He was enjoying the stimulus of living in close contact both with the university and the cathedral.

The parish was of the kind that might expect to have a Mirfield-trained curate. It was High Church, and the sung Eucharist was the main Sunday service. The vicar was Hilary Morse, who had been much influenced by Eric Milner-White at King's College Cambridge. Fr Morse ensured that the services were conducted immaculately and according to the English Use. This meant the 'Interim Rite'; a form of service beloved of those who, not wishing to use the Roman Catholic *Canon Missae,* nevertheless found the consecration prayer of the Book of Common Prayer unsatisfactory. Wishing to be, as they often described themselves in those days 'Prayer Book Catholics', they utilized the elements of the 1662 service but rearranged them in a way which they believed provided a 'Catholic' canon. The Prayer Book consecration prayer was followed immediately by the prayer of oblation (O Lord and heavenly Father, we thy humble servants entirely desire thy fatherly goodness mercifully to accept this our sacrifice of praise and thanksgiving) from the Prayer Book, bridged by the not insignificant word 'wherefore'. This extended and 'improved' consecration prayer was followed in turn by the Lord's Prayer. It was the form of eucharistic worship in which Ronald had taken part at Mirfield for five years (and most probably at Stoke Damerel) so it was not uncongenial to him.[2]

We have seen that music was important to Ronald, so he was fortunate in the fine musical tradition of St Oswald's. The church had a superb organist and a modern organ built by the local firm of Harrison and Harrison, who were recognized internationally as the builders of 'Rolls Royce' church organs. All this was most acceptable and comfortable. Yet curiously, it was something connected with the musical past of St Oswald's that stirred a new historical interest.

The most famous nineteenth-century vicar of St Oswald's had been John Bacchus Dyke, who was very much involved in the production of *Hymns Ancient and Modern.* It is often forgotten, in an age when 'Hymns A & M' might be looked back upon as the most common and generally acceptable hymnbook of the last generation, that in its day 'A & M' was very much a Party book – and the High Church Party at that. It was among the shibboleths which were used to test high or low church allegiance. Therefore, not only to be using, but also to be a contributor to this Tractarian volume, would be thought undeniable evidence of papistical sympathies! Consequently, the low-church Bishop of Durham (Dr Baring) did nothing to discourage a campaign of persecution against Dr Dykes over his High Church liturgical practices at St Oswald's.[3]

This piece of local history stimulated Ronald, he said, to take an interest in not only that particular parish's ritualistic trouble, but also all the upheaval, claim and counter-claim, heat and invective that occupied so much of the Church of England's energies in the second part of the nineteenth century. He also came to understand how these controversies had set in motion a process which led to the abortive attempts to revise the Prayer Book in 1927 and 1928.

From what we have already discovered about Ronald, we know that any such study would be neither facile nor cursory; it would entail applying the same standards of historical research of which Professor Hamilton Thompson had recognized he was capable. Two people encouraged him to work on this subject. The first was his Bishop, Dr Williams, who from the beginning showed a great deal of interest in what the curate of St Oswald's was doing. In due course, when Ronald began to write up his researches, the Bishop was kind enough to read through and comment on everything that Ronald wrote. Looking back on this many years later in 1990 he declared, 'It now seems incredible that a busy diocesan bishop should have been prepared to spend so much time and energy on a young curate.' But surely the Bishop had been shrewd enough to spot talent when he saw it.

The second person who encouraged the young curate was Colin Dunlop who in 1944 became Bishop of Jarrow – the Suffragan Bishopric of the Diocese of Durham. Dunlop was a keen liturgist, lent books to Ronald, and stimulated his latent interest in the subject. This early contact with Colin Dunlop proved to be of the greatest possible significance for Ronald Jasper. In 1949 Bishop Dunlop organized a Clergy School at Durham to commemorate the 400th anniversary of the first Prayer Book. Ronald Jasper was invited by Bishop Dunlop to be among the seven lecturers at this conference. The others, besides Bishop Dunlop himself, were Bishop Henry de Candole, D. E. W. Harrison, R. A. Beddoes, G. W. O. Addleshaw and A. S. Duncan-Jones. At the time Ronald's name must have seemed a surprising addition to such a distinguished team. When in 1955 the Archbishops of Canterbury and York agreed to the setting up of a Liturgical Commission, they asked Colin Dunlop (by then Dean of Lincoln) to be its first chairman, and all these other 1949 Durham lecturers (with the exception of Duncan-Jones who had died just a few months beforehand) were invited to be members. Indeed, the creation of such a body as 'a Liturgical Commission' was one of the topics which had been discussed at the Durham Clergy School in 1949, so, by 1955, things had come (almost) full circle.

Marriage

However, the days of the Liturgical Commission were still a few years away for the curate of St Oswald's, and although he continued diligently with his researches into the ritual controversies of the nineteenth century and those years of debate that preceded the production of the 1928 Prayer Book, there were personal matters which were now making claims on his time: specifically – the domestic science teacher from Ryhope.

Betty Wiggins was born at Seaham Harbour. After Seaham Grammar School, she went on to the Edinburgh College of Domestic Science. Having completed her training she went to teach at Ryhope. There was a domestic science centre situated in the church school which served the area around Ryhope.

It would seem that the new curate found his duties in the church school increasingly congenial and the young teacher found his attentions acceptable. None the less, their first date had to survive an anxious moment. They had arranged to meet at a cinema and at the agreed time Ronald was nowhere to be seen. Betty need not have worried, he was only slightly late, and after a few minutes rolled up in a shining, highly polished vehicle – a funeral hearse. He had come directly from the cemetery. On their second tryst, to see the film *Gone with the Wind*, Betty recalls that his transport was more conventional. They were married at St Oswald's, Durham on 10 August 1943.

Priest-in-charge at Langley Park and Esh

Ronald and Betty's first parish together was Esh, where at first Ronald had charge just of the district of Langley Park. But after only four months the Revd J. K. Hawke, who had been appointed priest-in-charge of Esh in the absence of the vicar on wartime chaplaincy duties, was forced by ill-health to retire, and so Ronald took charge of the whole parish. The newly-married couple stayed on in the parsonage at Langley Park.

The little village of Esh stands on a hill-ridge between the valley of the Browney and Deerness rivers, and Langley Park lies in the Browney valley to the north of Esh. The church at Esh (St Michael and All Angels) was founded at the end of the thirteenth century, rebuilt in 1770, and again in the nineteenth century. It stands by an ancient village green on the far side of which is Esh Hall, and alongside which are some houses and cottages. In the 1940s the population was about three hundred. The part of the parish called Langley Park grew up, not unlike Ryhope, in response to a pit. When the Jaspers arrived there it was a large thriving mining community with a population of nearly four thousand. All Saints' church at Langley Park was much larger than the parish church of St Michael at Esh.

Fifty years later, the Jasper time at Langley Park is not forgotten. One former parishioner Ella Wright recalls: 'Apart from being a sad time, as it was in the war years, it was a happy time in the local church. Ron and Betty were a hard-working couple, popular with young and old alike. A rather dour Churchwarden, somewhat difficult at first I remember, soon became very supportive.' The young priest-in-charge started a parish leaflet which he said would provide a means of letting parishioners know: (a) What has been done in the Parish (b) What it is hoped to do (c) What opportunities for worship and instruction are provided. The leaflet contains evidence of a great deal of parochial activity: Mothers' Union, Men's Circle, Sunday school, youth work. One of the earliest visiting preachers that Ronald invited to Esh was the Van Mildert Professor from Durham – Canon Michael Ramsey. The parish leaflet does not contain any reference to liturgical changes made by Ronald. He seems to have maintained the *status quo*.

This parish of Ronald's had a flourishing 'Fellowship of Youth', and Enid Eccleston who still lives in Langley Park, remembers Ronald producing *A Midsummer Night's Dream* with members of this club. Enid writes, 'I remember how well he served the parish during the difficult war years and we were very sorry to see him go.' Contemporary evidence of this last fact can be found in a letter he specially preserved: 'On this, the eve of your departure from us to St Giles, I would like to express my appreciation to you, and to Mrs Jasper for all that you have done for the good of All Saints' Church, during your short time with us, for your interest and efforts for the Organisations of our Church, the Mothers' Union, Youth Fellowship, Sunday School, and Choir not forgetting the small, but happy, Men's Circle; and the very important work of attending and administering to the sick of the Parish.' Ronald himself said to the people of Esh and Langley Park on his departure, 'I must ask for forgiveness if, as a result of inexperience, weakness or mistakes on my part, the parish or individual members of it have not received the ministrations expected from a parish priest. May God grant you all every happiness and blessing in the future.'

The need for Ronald to move on was caused by the return of the vicar of the parish, Cyril Blomeley, who had been serving as a chaplain to the Forces. One of Ronald's Mirfield contemporaries recalls that he had expressed an interest in serving as a chaplain to the Forces. In March 1945 the Bishop of Durham wrote to a number of clergy (was it those serving as curates?) to say that he had been asked 'urgently to provide a list of clergy who might, after the end of the war, be able to minister abroad for a special term of service – possibly a year – to the occupying troops'. The idea was that this would facilitate the release of those chaplains who had already given very long service or who were specially needed at home. Ronald was interested in the idea.

There was also a possibility that Ronald might go to a lectureship at St Andrew's University, but the Bishop of Durham was not keen on the idea and advised against it. The Bishop hoped that he might find a place 'where you could better combine the teaching work with directly ministerial work. After the war I fully expect that there will be a good many teaching posts which would offer this possibility, and I would give you all the help I could in this matter.' The Bishop wrote that he would not stand in Ronald's way, and that he could go ahead and apply to St Andrew's, but that if nothing came of it, it would not be too late to offer to go abroad as a chaplain. In the event, neither of these options was taken up because in July 1945 the Bishop asked him to go as curate in charge of St Giles Durham for a year. This was first discussed when the Bishop gave Ronald a lift in his car to a conference at Consett, but he emphasized that it would be necessary first of all to obtain the consent of the Dean and

Chapter of Durham who were Patrons of St Giles. This was duly obtained, and the Jaspers moved from Langley Park into the twenty-seven-roomed St Giles Vicarage, where they occupied the two middle floors. Betty remembers that it was bitterly cold.

Curate-in-charge of St Giles Durham

Gilesgate is on the east side of Durham, with St Giles church set in the most populous part of the city. On arrival, Ronald's attitude towards parish strategy seems to have been markedly different from that at Esh and Langley Park. Now he was not content to maintain things as they had always been, for at St Giles 'innovation' was the name of the game. Once again he introduced a parish magazine, but the first issue tells parishioners of changes to come. Of particular interest, having in mind his future work and achievements, was his announcement that he had commenced, with the agreement of the Parochial Church Council (PCC), a 'Parish Communion' each Sunday at 9 a.m. 'There will be hymns and a very short address on the Collect for the day – the whole service not taking more than 35 minutes. It is intended for everyone – old and young, confirmed and unconfirmed – so that the whole parish is able to join together at a reasonable hour for the Church's central act of worship. This service has made an encouraging start,' he reported to the St Giles congregation, 'and I hope that more people will get the "9 a.m. habit".'

At his second PCC meeting Ronald told members he had discovered a set of vestments in a cupboard in the vestry 'many of them beautifully worked by former parishioners'. It was decided that they could be brought back into use immediately. He also introduced a parish meeting. This was not the PCC, it was a meeting open to all parishioners, not just to an elected few. The idea was advocated by those who promoted the concept of Parish Communion. Ideally, they believed that just as the congregation meets together on a Sunday to share in the Eucharist, they ought to meet each week to share their thoughts and ideas on the Church and its mission.[4] St Giles did not achieve this ideal of a weekly meeting, but there were regular parish meetings throughout Ronald's short time in the parish. Additionally, and within three months of his arrival, he organized a teaching week for the congregation at which baptismal policy and 'other questions such as Confession, Holy Communion were dealt with'. He also introduced the Christmas crib; a Nativity

Play; the Three Hours Service on Good Friday; and held baptisms within the normal Sunday services, rather than 'hole-in-the-corner' affairs on a Sunday afternoon.

This whirlwind of activity suited some, but not all, the parishioners of St Giles. Miss Elsie Akenhead remembers that Ronald conducted services with dignity and feeling; that he was an extremely clear speaker who did not waste words, and got to the point without padding or embroidery. She also remembers that, 'As usual a minority did not care for his forthright manner.' That this was true is reflected in the minutes of a special meeting of the PCC held on 1 July 1946 (just before he left) at which the subject of some recognition of his ministry at St Giles was discussed. In a secret ballot they voted thirteen to six against a 'presentation' but twelve to seven in favour of 'a letter of appreciation'.[5]

The Jaspers and the Bishop of Durham realized that the appointment at St Giles was no more than a stop-gap, and that a more substantial post was needed. Letters about this went backwards and forwards, to and from Auckland Castle. One offer was declined and Ronald was worried that the Bishop might be annoyed about this. Dr Williams assures him that he was not. 'I strongly believe,' the Bishop kindly says, 'except in very rare cases, it is seldom right to attempt to press a man who has come to a clearly negative mind, and I accept your decision. I shall be glad if you will for the present "carry on".' Later, the Bishop again reassures him, 'I don't quite know why you have felt the last few months "a bad patch". I don't think that will have been the impression in the parish.' Whether or not it was a 'bad patch' (and we have seen that his time at St Giles did have its problems), it was certainly a worrying one. An appointment of a new rector for St Giles (Jack Norwood) had been made and so it was clear that Ronald's work there had to come to an end. The Bishop accepted the urgency of the situation and wrote saying that he only asked for a reassurance that Ronald wished to stay in the diocese and would 'consider formally any suggestion'. In a letter dated 28 May the Bishop noted that there were one or two places in the diocese, notably South Shields, where help was urgently needed.

Chaplain at the University of Durham

It was now that a vacancy for a chaplain at University and Hatfield Colleges thankfully occurred. Ronald immediately applied, backed by recommendations from his teachers at Leeds University, and was chosen. The Bishop was pleased with the appointment and wrote to say that he was 'very glad that you are going to do this very important University work'. He hoped that he would see a good deal of him 'for I get to the Castle quite often though not nearly as often as I should like'. The Castle at Durham was part of the University.

There is no doubt that Ronald was a popular and successful chaplain as far as the undergraduates were concerned, but unfortunately he did not believe that he received wholehearted support from the Master, Lt-Col Angus Alexander Macfarlane-Grieve MC, MA, and did not stay in the job as long as he would have liked. Even so, the Master wrote in *Castellum*, the university magazine, that the chaplain and another resident tutor had done so well 'that he wondered however we got on without them'.[6]

Fr Allan Grainge SSJE was an undergraduate at the time and tells how Ronald worked hard with the students despite all the difficulties. At that time the chaplain had not only the two colleges (University and Hatfield) to care for, but also had to cope with the fact that, because of the increased numbers of undergraduates after the war, students in their first year were being housed in another castle, Lumley Castle, which was just outside Chester-le-Street, some eight miles from Durham.

By this time Ronald and Betty had had their first child, Christine. They lived in somewhat spartan conditions at Cosin's Hall. Betty recalls with distaste the mice and cockroaches, while Fr Grainge remembers feeling fortunate that at Lumley Castle they had central heating, which the Jaspers did not. Certainly not in 1947 he says, when in Durham the year started with a snowfall which did not thaw until the middle of March!

But all was not cold and misery in Durham, as Fr Grainge remembers:

> In the Michaelmas term of 1947 we moved into Durham and had rooms in the Castle. Those of us who wished attended Mattins and Evensong in the College Chapel and went to the early Eucharist in the Cathedral. Mattins was at 8.40 a.m. and my one vivid memory is of Ash Wednesday. Ronald had decided that we ought to say the Litany following Mattins and in order not to prolong the service, as some of us had lectures at 9 a.m., said that we would finish Mattins after the Benedictus and follow with the Litany. Dr Pace, who at one time had

been Vice Chancellor and was extremely deaf, was a regular member of the congregation. We finished the Benedictus and Ronald announced that we would now say the Litany. Dr Pace, under the impression that we were going on as usual immediately said in a loud voice 'Christ have mercy upon us'. Ronald managed to retain his composure – the rest of us didn't!

Incumbent at Stillington

There were other happy occasions during their time at the university for the Jaspers to look back on. Such was the baptism of Christine, which took place in Durham Castle Chapel on 21 February 1947 with the Bishop of Durham officiating – though at first a licence was lacking and Ronald had to persuade the college authorities to find the required fee of one guinea. Over the tea which followed the service, the Bishop must have picked up that Ronald was not happy in his work at the college. Writing to Ronald a few days later the Bishop says: 'I was not at all surprised to hear from you, for you have been much in my mind, and I am actively considering a job for you and have only been waiting for dates and places to come a little more clearly out of the mist . . . But I can say now that I expect to have an offer to make to you . . . I hope this move will help you.'

The following Saturday, 8 May 1947, Ronald went to Auckland Castle. The Bishop offered him the parish of Heatherycleugh in Bishop Auckland, but within a few days Ronald decided to decline the offer. It would seem that during the Saturday interview the Bishop had mentioned the possibility of another parish – Stillington near Stockton-on-Tees. This seemed a more interesting prospect to Ronald, but the Bishop had told him that he was not yet in a position to offer it to him. He needed to wait to see if the Stillington PCC had any representations they wished to make about their new vicar. The Jaspers had not long to wait. In a letter of 5 June marked 'Confidential' the Bishop gave him the good news that in a month's time he would be able to nominate to Stillington. The Bishop was as good as his word, and a formal offer was made to Ronald on 17 July. The service of admission to the Perpetual Curacy of Stillington was held on Friday, 1 October 1948.

AN INDUSTRIAL VILLAGE

When Ronald arrived at Stillington it could be described as a tiny industrial island in a sea of south-east Durham farmland. It lay in the shadow of iron slagheaps which stretched along the entire width of the village. Factory chimneys were still emitting smoke and from a distance it did not seem unlike the other pit villages. Once in the village, however, Stillington could be seen to be different. There were rows of well-kept allotments, and off the road through the village led broad streets of sturdy, clean houses of grey stone and red brick, or just red brick. Behind these was a park with flowerbeds, shady trees and a war memorial.

Even so, Stillington had experienced its share of ups and downs. The Carlton Iron Works, which had employed the best part of the male population, had closed down in 1930. But Stillington refused to die. For many years the men existed on the dole, and scraps of occasional work. The park, which had been laid out in the first place by the Carlton Ironworks, using the excess profits which would otherwise have gone to the exchequer (or so the villagers maintained), was improved and maintained by voluntary labour. Being surrounded by farming country and farming traditions meant that many of the Stillington residents kept livestock as well as allotments. This came in useful in times of depression, with the result that although during those hard times there was some migration out of the village, very few of the houses were left unoccupied.

Work slowly filtered back to Stillington. First was the slag wool-works, utilizing the iron left from the Carlton days. By the 1950s it employed about one hundred men and women. Others travelled to Billingham to work for ICI. But the unemployment which had disappeared during the war, reappeared during Ronald's incumbency. In August 1949 Ronald was interviewed by *The Northern Echo* who asked him about Stillington. What were they like, the people of this isolated industrial community? he was asked. He told the newspaper that they were progressive. 'It is a unique village and a pretty go-ahead one, too,' Vicar Jasper replied. Church attendance, he reckoned, was comparatively high. In a village of between 700 to 800 people there were never less than thirty at the Sunday morning service. The reporter told his readers that since the arrival of the new vicar there had been a number of new activities in the parish. 'After a nativity play at Christmas and a Passion play at

Easter Mr Jasper and his wife intend to expand and produce ordinary plays and also to form a group for folk song and dancing.' *The Northern Echo* observed that there was certainly plenty of life in a village that refused to lie down after the death sentence pronounced twenty years before. 'It is also a fair proof that industrialisation need not necessarily mean ribbon development, ugliness and dirt.'[7]

Ronald stayed at Stillington for seven years. It was to prove to be the major parochial assignment of his career. In that post-war period, church life in many such places was reasonably buoyant. It is true, as Paul Welsby has written in his *History of the Church of England 1945–1980*, that in the immediate aftermath of the war, the Church changed comparatively little.

> It is true that moderate alterations had been made in the parochial system and that heroic efforts had been made to cope with the needs of new housing areas, the repair of war damage, the demands of the Education Act and the financial problems of the clergy, but in many ways it was a Church sailing on an even keel, content with the old tried ways and the conventional orthodoxies. There was an atmosphere of complacency and an apparent unawareness of trends already present which were to burst to the surface in the sixties.[8]

In one particular aspect, which was to emerge as his major task for the Church, the Vicar of Stillington was carefully, but unknowingly, preparing himself to tackle the challenge of the sixties – and beyond.

LITURGICAL STUDY

Ronald continued the scholarly work that he had commenced when motivated by the parochial history of St Oswald's Durham. He was now studying in detail the efforts to revise the Book of Common Prayer during the nineteenth century. He did not spend time on the famous and unhappy ritual cases which were one of the scandals of the Church in that century. They were considered only insofar as they affected possible changes in the text of the Prayer Book. It was the proposed textual amendments which interested him.

In the first place, Ronald believed, it was necessary to make the point that the desire for a revision of the Prayer Book never died out, even after the abortive attempt in 1689. At that time suggestions were made for changes in the Prayer Book which, it was hoped, would comprehend and mollify the dissenters. Although this specific attempt at 'liturgical comprehension' failed there were always other suggestions around.[9] The general passion for reform at the beginning of the nineteenth century gave some of these campaigns new vigour. Then came the Oxford Movement.

The Tractarians, in their first years, were pretty well 'Prayer Book Fundamentalists'. The earliest *Tracts for the Times* contained spirited defences of the Prayer Book. In Tract Three, 'Thoughts on Alterations to the Liturgy', its author (John Henry Newman himself), encouraged the clergy to resist every attempt to secure alterations. Newman argued that of the proposed alterations, the limited number which would please a few would pain many. Only later in the more ritualistic stages did the nineteenth-century High Church movement start to press for changes in the text of the services, sometimes by making actual alterations in services, but mainly by adding to them from another source. Not to mince words – that source was Rome.[10] The result was not only the Ritual Trials but also the setting up of a Royal Commission on Ritual in 1867. All this may seem surprising in these faithless days – that a complicated machinery of state should be geared up to examine in detail the worship taking place in parish churches up and down the country. Yet this is what happened and Ronald examined it all. But for all their efforts, the so-called 'lawlessness' continued. In fact it was probably encouraged by the attempt to suppress it. There is nothing like creating a few martyrs (as did the Trials), to strengthen the resolve of the rank and file. Even ordinary parishioners felt themselves persecuted and closed ranks in acts of defiance against what they perceived as the intolerance of bishops, Protestant witch hunts, and parliamentary critics.

The developing liturgist

All this work, which Ronald undertook on the liturgical upheavals of the nineteenth century, was ordered into a thesis which he submitted to the University of Leeds for the degree of Bachelor of Divinity. And on 30 June 1950, Ronald was presented for the degree by Professor L. E. Browne in Leeds Town Hall. His next task was to do all that is necessary to 'de-thesisize' such a piece of work in order that it might be suitable for publication.[11] He did not accomplish that until June 1953, for in the meanwhile he had commenced another project.

In 'My development as a Liturgist' Ronald explains how this new project was the result of a suggestion by the Bishop of Jarrow (Colin Dunlop). The idea was that he tackle the editing of the liturgical correspondence of Walter Howard Frere, and prepare a volume for publication. This would be a logical continuation of Ronald's previous work on the eighteenth- and nineteenth-century liturgical upheavals. The upshot of those convoluted controversies about the worship of the Church of England, was that in 1904 the government of the day set up a further commission, the Royal Commission on Ecclesiastical Discipline. Within two years the Commission reported its opinion: 'the law of public worship in the Church of England is too narrow for the religious life of the present generation' and recommended that Letters of Business be given to the Convocations so that they might begin the task of producing revised services which would be more acceptable to the folk of a new century.

THE CHURCH'S EARLIER LITURGICAL REFORMS

One of the most influential books that appeared in the years immediately after the time of the Royal Commission's report was Frere's *Some Principles of Liturgical Reform.* In this, Frere prefaced his own suggestion with a plea that any revision should be in skilled hands. 'The serious work will only begin when the Convocations decide that it is at least as crucial a matter to revise the Prayer Book as to retranslate the Bible; and therefore are content to place the initial responsibility in the hands, not of a Committee of Convocation, which, except in the Upper House, contains few of the scholars who are most competent for the work, but a body of revisers gathered and empowered for the purpose.'[12]

Frere's suggestion was partly met in 1911. The Archbishop of Canterbury (Davidson) suggested the need for a body of experts to edit and co-ordinate the proposals which would ultimately come from the Houses of Convocation (Canterbury and York). It ought, the Archbishop thought, to be a small body, and representative of all schools of thought within the Church. Subsequently, Frere's fellow Community of the Resurrection pioneer Charles Gore (then Bishop of Birmingham) proposed the appointment by the Archbishops of 'a committee of scholars of acknowledged weight, whose advice can be sought with regard to liturgical and other proposals with which

Convocation is now dealing, and that Committees of this House be instructed to ask for such advice in all appropriate cases'. Frere was duly appointed to 'The Advisory Committee on Liturgical Questions' as it was called. He then continued to be involved in all the details of liturgical reform up to and including the proposals of 1927 and 1928.

RONALD EDITS FRERE

It was all these papers that Ronald examined, sifted and edited, acquiring as he did unrivalled knowledge of the intricacies of the debates and conferences which were the result of this detailed liturgical work, and of the vast correspondence it generated. No matter that they were the papers of a Mirfield Father, the Community to which Ronald owed so much – that was a bonus. The work followed on splendidly from his nineteenth-century studies and rounded things off, even if the conclusion was the 1927–28 parliamentary débâcle. At least he was able to identify the pitfalls and obstacles which lay in the path of those who might attempt such liturgical revision in the future. By no stretch of imagination could Ronald Jasper have realized, as he worked on Dr Frere's papers in his study at Stillington Vicarage, or in the library at Mirfield, that he would soon be at the eye of a similar storm himself, and personally involved in corresponding liturgical debates and discussions. As we shall see, many of the lessons had not been learned. And although this Vicar of Stillington had carefully and diligently flagged up the pitfalls, he was to see the Church of England ready to fall headlong into them.

Although by the time Ronald started his studies at Mirfield Frere had been dead for six months, he may well have seen and spoken to him on earlier visits from Leeds to Mirfield. They may also have come across each other in the south-west. Ronald reminisced: 'Colin Dunlop . . . lent me books and eventually suggested that I might do some work on Walter Frere, the former Bishop of Truro, who was probably of his day the Church's most eminent ecumenical and liturgical scholar, and one of the creators of the ill-fated 1928 Prayer Book. I had the singular good fortune to know him. As a boy and a young man, I had lived in Plymouth – just across the river Tamar from the diocese of Truro. With family connections in the diocese, and knowing some of his clergy well, I realised they held him in high regard and affection.'[13]

Ronald Jasper would never have claimed to be the same kind of liturgical scholar as Bishop Frere, but he certainly followed in his footsteps as an advocate of the necessity for scholarship to work alongside pastoral need in the revision of the liturgy of the Church of England. He learnt much from his work on the Frere papers and often referred to them.

His friend and mentor Fr Hannay CR, who was by now Bishop of Argyll and the Isles, took a particular interest in the Frere book, having known Walter Frere well. Thanking Ronald for sending him a copy, he wrote: 'I am delighted to have it both for your sake and +Walter's. Congratulations on a good job of work. I feel a sort of reflected glory; not that I ever taught you one word of liturgiology, but you are one of my dear sons.' Incidentally, it is about this time that Bishop Hannay stopped calling him 'Claud' in his letters. This had started at the Hostel in Leeds and was the nickname (if baptismal names can be called such) which he carried with him to Mirfield. But these things linger on, and even a few years later Fr Andrew Blair (the Prior at Mirfield) wrote saying, 'I really *must* stop this Claud business: it's like using baby language!'

PARISH ACTIVITIES

Life in the parish of Stillington was not all academic research and writing for Ronald Jasper; all the tasks and duties of the parochial ministry had to be fulfilled, such as services, administration, pastoral offices, visiting, caring and listening. Once again, as at Langley Park, he decided to employ his interest in drama and music to build up fellowship in the parish. It was that particularly English combination of words and music, the Savoyard operas of Gilbert and Sullivan, which were chosen as a vehicle for the parish's stage enterprises. The Stillington Parish Players performed *Trial by Jury*, *The Sorcerer*, *The Mikado* and *The Gondoliers*. Many of those taking part had never sung in public before and the vicar-cum-producer appealed in the printed programme for the audience to encourage the players as much as they could. The performance of *The Gondoliers* in March 1955 – just before the Jaspers left - was performed in the newly-opened Institute Hall in Stillington. In the opinion of the local newspaper, only those most closely connected with the social life of the district could fully appreciate how much was owed to Ronald's enthusiasm and encouragement. 'He was – and this is said in the nicest sense – a veritable Pooh-Bah. He trained the chorus, produced, directed, conducted and even erected the stage.'

If the world is a village, what is the Church of England within it? Conversations between churchpeople quickly identify parishes, churches, and certainly clergy, that they have in common. So that the criss-crossing of relationships within the Church is not as surprising as it must seem – coincidences will happen. Consider, then, this item in the Stillington parish magazine for April 1954 in which the vicar says: 'A month or so ago I received an official receipt for our contribution to the Westminster Abbey Appeal Fund: but since then I have received a personal letter from Canon Carpenter of the Abbey thanking us for our donation. Other parishes have received similar letters of thanks, and this kindly and courteous act on the part of the Abbey Chapter is one which we should appreciate.' Fourteen years later, Canon (later Dean) Edward Carpenter would be one of Ronald's capitular colleagues with whom he would share responsibility for the restoration of the fabric of the Abbey.

FURTHER LITURGICAL RESEARCH

At Stillington there were further opportunities for Ronald's engagement in historical research. Between 1951 and 1954 he worked on the early life of Bishop Cosin. It is likely that his interest in Cosin arose out of the fact that the house in which he lived during his chaplaincy at Durham University was named Cosin's Hall.

John Cosin (1594–1672) was an eminent member of the Laudian school at the time of Charles I. Although born in Norwich, his ministry included two spells in the Durham diocese. He was a Canon of the Cathedral from 1625 to 1635, and in 1660, after the Restoration, was made Bishop of Durham. His High Church principles were opposed by the Puritans and he was deprived by the Long Parliament on account of his 'Popish innovations.' Restored to favour as Bishop of Durham, he attended the Savoy Conference of 1661, trying in vain to bring about a reconciliation between the Church of England and the Presbyterians. To this end he had prepared *The Durham Book*, a folio copy of the Book of Common Prayer with manuscript annotations in the margins and between the lines.[14]

The definitive edition of this first draft of the revision of the Book of Common Prayer in 1661 was edited by Dr Geoffrey Cuming for his Oxford DD in 1961. Dr Cuming became Ronald's vice-chairman for the Liturgical Commission – and one of his most trusted friends and advisers. Ronald's work on Cosin resulted in an article 'Some notes on the early life of Bishop John Cosin' published in the Durham diocese magazine *Bishopric* in November 1954. While working on Cosin, he made contact with Nikolaus Pevsner, the architectural historian, who had just begun his monumental series of guides, *The Buildings of England.* Pevsner was planning his volume on Durham, and Ronald contributed information about the work of Cosin, which Dr Pevsner acknowledged (in a letter of 14 January 1952) as containing 'points of importance'.

Ronald's article in the *Bishopric* was warmly welcomed by the new Bishop of Durham, Michael Ramsey. Bishop Ramsey was an old friend, having been Professor at Durham from 1940 to 1950. On leaving Durham in 1950 to take up the Regius Chair at Cambridge, Michael Ramsey wrote to Ronald: 'It was always very delightful in those last years to see you and have the chance of some talk, and I shall in future be hoping to see you sometimes and get news of your doings. We really do hate leaving Durham.' Events decreed that not only would they soon work again in Durham (Michael Ramsey only stayed two years in Cambridge and was consecrated as Bishop of Durham in York Minster on Michaelmas Day 1952) but later when Ramsey reached Lambeth there would be even more intimate co-operation.

Then came an unexpected commission. Ronald was asked to write the biography of Arthur Cayley Headlam. Headlam had been Principal, Dean and Professor of Dogmatic Theology at King's College, London before being Regius Professor of Divinity at Oxford, and then Bishop of Gloucester. Bishop Headlam was much involved in the ecumenical movement. Ronald was delighted at the prospect of starting this work; he often said that of all the possible alternatives the writing of ecclesiastical biographies would have been his personally chosen vocation – but the Church was to decide otherwise.

Preparing to move on

On the strength of his work on the Prayer Book Revision, his editing of the Frere correspondence, plus various articles, Ronald Jasper was elected to a Fellowship of the Royal Historical Society in 1954. His application for the Fellowship was supported by A.T.P. Williams, now Bishop of Winchester, and Canon Claude Jenkins, Fellow of Christ Church Oxford.

Here then, was a rising star. With two higher degrees under his belt, and two widely regarded books and a series of monographs written, he could not long be disregarded by those who made ecclesiastical appointments.

Two particular opportunities to move from Stillington presented themselves, the first coming after only four years, but considering Ronald's interest and expertise it could not altogether have surprised him. Early in 1952 he was asked if he would allow his name to be considered for appointment as Vicar of St Mary's Primrose Hill, in north-west London.

Roger Lloyd refers to St Mary's in *The Church of England 1900–1965*:

> It was natural that one of the foremost places in the history of the development of public worship during this period should be occupied by a priest who owed almost everything to the Catholic revival, and yet was strongly opposed to many of its latter-day manifestations. This priest was Percy Dearmer, Vicar of St Mary's, Primrose Hill, in London. He had the two expressions of real genius which gave him a commanding place in the revival of worship as a fine art. He had the gift of persuading the most unlikely people to work together, and of holding them to the task until it was done; and he was a true artist, with an artist's selective enthusiasm and the gift of taking endless pains over matters of detail. St Mary's gave him a sphere of his own in which all his principles could be worked out and tried in the actual conditions of parish life. The result was that not only his parishioners but also many pilgrims from all over the country could see an order of worship which was genuinely English and correctly Catholic. In hardly another church could just the same thing be seen, for Dearmer was unique in his knowledge of the principles and precedents of worship.[15]

Unfortunately, at the time that Ronald was asked to consider the appointment, things at Primrose Hill were not at their happiest. One of the trustees was Bishop Colin Dunlop, whose name would coincide with Ronald's yet again in a few years; he was obviously responsible for this invitation. Bishop Dunlop had been a curate to Arthur

Duncan-Jones (who succeeded Dearmer) at St Mary's, and is guarded in his comments in a personal letter to Ronald. Replying to some of Ronald's questions, one of which was about continuing his researches and studies while at Primrose Hill, he states that the competition for 'supplementary academic work' in London would be very high. In the event Ronald did not go to St Mary's. Both the Bishop and Bishop-designate thought this was right. A. T. P. Williams said, 'I am glad myself that you will not be leaving the diocese – yet at any rate.' And Michael Ramsey wrote from Cambridge, responding to a letter of congratulation on being appointed as Bishop of Durham: 'We love Durham, and will be happy to be back. I am glad now that you did not go to Primrose Hill!'

Twelve months later in October 1953, came another attempt to lure him away from Stillington, this time overseas. The suggestion came from the Community of the Resurrection. The Community had the patronage of St John's Church Territet, at Vand in Switzerland. The congregation consisted mainly of elderly people who lived in or near Montreux, but the age-level was regularly lowered by the existence of two schools for girls in the vicinity. During the season there were a large number of visitors, and the congregation also contained a 'trickle' of Anglo-Swiss citizens. It had, in the ecclesiastical jargon of the time, 'full Catholic privileges': sung Mass (using the Interim Rite) on Sunday, the Blessed Sacrament reserved, and confessions heard. Ronald took the offer seriously; for one thing he asked his friend Miss Persis Wingfield to investigate St George's School Montreux as a possible place for Christine to continue her studies. More importantly, he turned again to his own Bishop and to his former college principal – the Primus of the Scottish Episcopal Church.

Michael Ramsey sent him a long, handwritten (and, as always, barely decipherable) letter. Only if Ronald felt drawn to the distinctive kind of pastoral (plus rather vague ecumenical) work which the Chaplaincy at Montreux afforded, should he go, the Bishop says. He then discusses at length the possibilities for Ronald continuing his literary work in Switzerland. 'I think that the opportunities there for literary work are likely to be in some ways better and in other ways worse than in England. *Pro*, a little more time; *con*, lack of contact with books and libraries. So I think the decision turns on the job itself rather than on its ancillary opportunities.' In that same letter Bishop Ramsey mulls over the opportunities for a priest to write while faithfully fulfilling his other tasks. No doubt drawing on his own experiences, Michael Ramsey is of the opinion that there are really no posts where literary work can be pursued without the tensions of other responsibilities. 'This is equally true of parishes, academic posts and communities.' The Bishop believed that the Jaspers should move from Stillington before too long , but offers some typical Ramsey wisdom. 'I greatly hope for you that a change from Stillington may come: because the *quality* of Stillington is such that your wife and you should move after these years there. But any move, while freeing you from the peculiar *quality* of Stillington, would leave you with about the same *quantity* of other duties alongside literary work.' Ramsey then concludes with an aphorism which all authors, not least Ronald in the succeeding years, would take to heart: 'Books are always written amid factors which conflict to make it impossible!'

Probably on the very same day a letter arrived from St Bride's Onich in Lanarkshire in which the Most Reverend the Primus is even more directive. He has heard about the Swiss offer through his Mirfield contacts. 'Fools rush in where angels fear to tread! It is none of my business, but I have seen various letters about St John's Territet and I have an affectionate interest in all that concerns you.' The Primus hopes that Ronald would give due weight, in pondering the matter, to his writing and study. As we have seen from Ronald's correspondence with Michael Ramsey, he was doing just that. His resolve must have been strengthened when he read that Fr Hannay thought: 'So few clergy today have the taste or ability for study, that I should be sorry if you were hindered. You wrote in your letter to the Prior (about the offer of Territet) that you had a strong sense of vocation on that side. Don't let it be smothered by other considerations however excellent, but give it due weight.'

Fr Hannay later wrote, when Ronald had told him that he had decided not to go to Territet, to say that he felt sure the decision was right. During the following year Michael Ramsey made a number of suggestions for a move within the Diocese. Ronald had quite firmly made up his mind to leave Stillington and go on somewhere which would afford him more time for writing. At one time West Hartlepool seemed a possibility. The Bishop wrote: 'It will give you a chance to give a good deal of time to literary work. Your acceptance would also strengthen the Church in West Hartlepool in ways as real as they are hard precisely to define.' So if it was to be neither

Primrose Hill, West Hartlepool nor the mountains of Switzerland – where next then?

The move to Exeter

SUCCENTOR AT THE CATHEDRAL

The young eighteen-year-old Ronald Jasper had left Plymouth for the unknown north of England twenty years previously, and now came the opportunity to return to the south-west and his native diocese of Exeter. He was appointed as Succentor of Exeter Cathedral. Of his appointment Bishop Ramsey wrote (8 June 1955): 'So be it. I am glad that you are going to a place where you will have great scope for some of the things which you are called to do. I cannot say how sorry I am that we shall have you in Durham no longer.'

In 705 the West-Saxon bishopric founded by Birinus and centered at Dorchester was divided, and a new bishopric with its See at Sherborne was founded. Subsequently, this diocese was divided by Archbishop Plegmund of Canterbury in 909, and a new diocese of Crediton was established. In 1050, owing to the exposure of Crediton to the ravages of pirates, Leofric, Bishop of Crediton, with the approval of Leo IX, moved the See to Exeter. There was already a Benedictine monastery there, but nothing remains of it and the oldest parts of the present cathedral are post-conquest, dating from AD 1112 to 1150. The thirteenth- and fourteenth-century building was restored by George Gilbert Scott in the 1870s. The cathedral has been described as an exuberant building, containing the longest unbroken line in the Gothic style of vaulting anywhere.[16] Ronald Jasper came to love the building and to enjoy his part in conducting and organizing the worship within it.

In May 1955, Bishop Surtees, as Precentor, organized interviews and voice trials for the candidates, the result of which was a unanimous decision to offer Ronald a position in the cathedral.

The chapter minutes for 4 June 1955 record his appointment as priest-vicar, succentor, sub-treasurer and sacrist, and a week later states that he would reside temporarily at 14 The Close. He was installed at Evensong on 26 September when the service was sung to 'Wesley in F' – the composition of a former Exeter organist, S. S. Wesley, who also held the office of succentor. The Jaspers moved in

March 1956 into Palace Gate House. About this time, in addition to his duties in the cathedral, Ronald was appointed assistant master at the cathedral school.

Up until 1933 there had been a College of Vicars Choral at Exeter. Like many other similar cathedral bodies, they were jealous of this distinction from the Dean and Chapter. As Prebendary R. C. B. Llewellyn observes in his article 'Fifty Years at Exeter Cathedral' for the *Friends Report* of 1957, 'They had certain rights and privileges which the Dean and Chapter did not control.' The compulsory handing over of their property and endowments in 1933 was 'a sad end to a very old foundation which had existed since 1050 and had possessed a Royal Charter granted them on 26 February 1401'.[17] Barely twenty years later, when Ronald arrived in Exeter, this tradition of independence was not altogether dead. Dr John Thurmer, who worked in the Diocese of Exeter for twenty-seven years (of which nearly twenty were as a Canon of the Cathedral) writes that the liturgical distinction between the priest vicars and the chapter was still observed until 1972. The primary duty of the priest-vicar was to officiate at the daily offices, said or sung. In those days 'I doubt if a Canon ever officiated at statutory mattins or evensong,' says Canon Thurmer.

The Latin word *succinere* means to sing, to accompany, chime in, agree. In the late Middle Ages a cathedral succentor was a kind of sub-chanter. He took up the chant after the precentor (pre-chanter) and led the chanting. The succentor presided over the left choir and the precentor over the right. The office of succentor soon developed into a precentor's deputy in an old-foundation cathedral, because the precentor was a member of the cathedral chapter and was often called away on other ecclesiastical duties.

At Exeter, up until 1933, the office and its responsibilities was filled by several members of the College of Lay Vicars. Indeed, S. S. Wesley who was appointed organist of Exeter Cathedral in 1835, was also the succentor, being part of the College of Lay Vicars. Prior to 1933 there was no necessity for the succentor to be ordained.

Ronald Jasper's terms of reference for his new job were clear. They were laid down in 'The Regulations made by the Dean and Chapter as to the office of Succentor'. They stated that: 'The Succentor is to be considered the representative of the Dean and Chapter in all matters connected with both the Regular and Voluntary Choirs. He derives all his authority directly from the Dean and Chapter, and will act under their direction and control. In all cases of doubt or difficulty he will at once refer to them for instructions.'

However, there was one important additional rule. The regulations stated that, 'In matters primarily musical he shall give due consideration to the judgement of the Organist.' During Ronald's time at Exeter there were problems with the relationship between the cathedral organist, Reginald Moore and the Dean and Chapter, in which it became the succentor's responsibility to mediate. Unfortunately, events resulted in the organist being dismissed. He was suceeded by Lionel Dakers who became a particular friend of Ronald's, a friendship which continued when Dr Dakers became Director of the Royal School of Church Music at Addington Palace.

Writing the Headlam biography

At Exeter, Ronald embarked upon a major piece of work. As we know, he had been commissioned to write the official biography of Arthur Cayley Headlam. Headlam was a Fellow of All Souls' who, after seven years as Vicar of Welwyn in the St Alban's Diocese, became a vigorous and energetic Principal of King's College London at a crucial point in the college's history. His skills as an administrator reshaped King's, and he was instrumental in designing the theological department there and founding the Faculty of Theology in the University of London – both of which were still very much as Headlam had intended when Ronald Jasper himself went to teach at King's in 1960. The more recent changes at King's were still a few years off even when Ronald left the college.

Even so, if in the invitation to write the Headlam biography we might be tempted, with the benefit of hindsight, to say that once again it seemed as though future events were being foreshadowed, that was far from the minds of the members of the Headlam family. They were choosing a rising ecclesiastical historian who would be emphathetic with his subject. The research would range over a large area. Although the Bishop had left a mass of documents and correspondence at the family home at Whorlton near Barnard Castle in County Durham, there was also Headlam's time as Regius Professor of Divinity at Oxford, and his subsequent and significant occupation of the See of Gloucester, to be covered by his biographer.

Ronald began the work before he left the north-east, and had acquired a good working knowledge of the Whorlton material. He also made the acquaintance of the Bishop's redoubtable sister, Miss Rose Headlam, and Headlam's nieces and literary executors Professor Agnes Headlam-Morley and Miss Persis Wingfield. Miss Wingfield was Betty's Principal at the Edinburgh College of Domestic Science. She was not merely a great encourager and enabler of the work, but also became a particular friend of the Jasper family. Hence the advice about schooling in Switzerland.

The writing of the biography of such a many-sided man – 'Erasmus Redivivus' he was called by more than one foreign churchman – involved many hours of careful and patient research. Headlam was an English churchman who made a great impression upon the developing ecumenical movement, and he had important contacts in various parts of Christendom. To these issues Headlam brought an acute theological mind which did not suffer fools gladly. In the foreword which he contributed to the biography, W. R. Matthews, one of the young men of King's College in which Headlam discovered promise, and who himself became Dean of King's before becoming Dean of St Paul's, commented: 'It has been said that a gentleman is one who is never rude except intentionally. This does not apply to Headlam. He could indeed be rude of set purpose. Towards the end of his life he came to see us at St Paul's after a meeting of Bishops at Lambeth and commented "I am getting deaf and that prevents me from being as rude as I should like to be!" But most often he was rude without intention.'

Family matters

While at Stillington, Ronald had made a rare trip to the south-west for his parent's golden wedding anniversary. He and Betty went on their own, 'an annoying dose of chicken pox' prevented the children joining them, but the event was of significance to Ronald and evoked an even rarer reference to family matters in the parish magazine. 'This celebration is a unique one for me, in that it is the first gathering of my own family that I have attended for the better part of twenty years. It makes one realise how short and transitory our life on this earth is. I suppose the older we get the things which are really eternal become more real – at least so I find it myself. And the reality of the Eternal does help keep us on an even keel in this topsy-turvy world in which we live.'

In December 1957, soon after the Jasper's had moved to Exeter, his mother Florence died after a distressing illness. Later his father Claud moved from Furneux Road to Watts Park Road in Peverell, Plymouth.

The children were growing up. Christine was at the Maynard School in Exeter, and in 1958 David had won through to the preparatory department of Exeter School. David was born in a nursing home in Stockton-on-Tees in 1951, while Ronald was still Vicar of Stillington. Betty had become well known as a lecturer in domestic science at schools and clubs. She was also busy as an examiner on this same subject for the London University Examination Board. As Ronald was also examining in scripture knowledge for the Joint Matriculation Board, there were times of the year when the postman was a greatly burdened visitor to Palace Gate House, which was almost snowed under by examination scripts.

However, it was not a communication from an examination board but from Lambeth Palace that was to change Ronald's life almost entirely and to set his feet upon the path which would ensure his enduring place in the history of the Church of England. It was an invitation from the Archbishop of Canterbury (Geoffrey Fisher) to be a founding member of the Liturgical Commission.

NOTES

1. Jasper, 'My development as a Liturgist', (ed. David Jasper), *The Friends of York Minster 62nd Annual Report 1991*, p. 17.
2. The 'Interim Rite' derived from the proposal made by Bishop A. Chandler in a letter to the *Church Times* on 2 January 1931 (see F. L. Cross, *Darwell Stone*, Westminster, 1943, pp. 216–17).
3. *Oxford Dictionary of the Christian Church*, (2 edn), Oxford, 1983, p. 436.
4. Donald Gray, *Earth and Altar*, Alcuin Club Collections no. 68, Norwich, 1986, pp. 143–5.
5. EP/DU SG 268, Durham Record Office
6. *Castellum*, no. 1, 1948, p. 6.
7. *The Northern Echo*, 6 August 1949, p. 3.
8. Paul A. Welsby, *A History of the Church of England 1945–1980*, Oxford, 1983, p. 94.
9. Timothy J. Fawcett, *The Liturgy of Comprehension 1689: An abortive attempt to revise the Book of Common Prayer*, Alcuin Club Collections no. 54, Southend-on-Sea, 1973. Dr Fawcett says in his preface: 'My thanks particularly are due to the Reverend Canon R. C. D. Jasper, who has guided my studies for many years as an undergraduate, postgraduate, and now author; and for the wealth of

experience he has put at my disposal, without which this book could never have been written.'

10. Peter B. Nockles, *The Oxford Movement in Context: Anglican High Churchmanship 1760–1857*, Cambridge, 1994, pp. 220–1.
11. Ronald Jasper, *Prayer Book Revision in England 1800–1900*, London, 1954.
12. W. H. Frere, *Some Principles of Liturgical Reform*, London, 1911, p. 8.
13. Jasper, 'My Development as a Liturgist', p. 18. The resulting book was: Ronald Jasper, *Walter Howard Frere, his Correspondence on Liturgical Revision and Construction*, Alcuin Club Collections no. 39, London, 1954.
14. G. J. Cuming, *The Durham Book, Being the First Draft of the Revision of the Book of Common Prayer in 1661*, Durham, 1961.
15. Roger Lloyd, *The Church of England 1900–1965*, London, 1966, p. 155.
16. Anthony New, *A Guide to the Cathedrals of Britain*, London, 1980, p. 159.
17. R. C. B. Llewellyn, 'Fifty Years at Exeter Cathedral', *Friends of Exeter Cathedral Report* (for year ending 31 March 1957), pp. 15–16.
18. Donald Hunt, *Samuel Sebastian Wesley*, Bridgend, 1990, pp. 25–8.
19. Ronald Jasper, *Arthur Cayley Headlam: The Life and Letters of a Bishop*, London, 1960, p. 9.

3

THE FORMATION OF THE LITURGICAL COMMISSION

BY VIRTUE OF writing a book on the history of nineteenth-century liturgical reform, and through editing the Frere liturgical correspondence, Ronald Jasper, the succentor of Exeter Cathedral, had acquired a unique overview of the most recent attempts by the Church of England to put its house in order as far as its worship was concerned. The attempts had not been successful; there was still a wide divergence of usage throughout the country, and a good deal of dissatisfaction with the narrow limits within which parishes had to work. He understood this, and had experienced these frustrations at the parochial level, where it really matters.

The Liturgical Movement

A SIMPLER EUCHARISTIC SERVICE?

These restrictions became more irksome as the fruits of the Liturgical Movement were assimilated in the parishes. As a result of the influence of the Oxford Movement there had been an increase in the frequency of Communion services, and in 'high' parishes the introduction of a Choral Communion, usually called the Sung Eucharist. But there was more to it than that in a significant number of parishes. For many years there had been those who realized that it was not merely of importance that the Eucharist be at the centre of parish life, but also that its communal and social dimensions should inform all the other work and witness of the church. This involved a simple and accessible Eucharist, held at an hour convenient for working people. (The only problem with a mid-morning timing was the issue of fasting communion, and this took too many years to sort out.) The style and content of these eucharistic services were very different from the Anglo-Catholic's High Mass or the Evangelical's 'High' Mattins.

'PARISH COMMUNION'

One of the earliest experiments was conducted by Ronald's liturgical 'hero', Walter Frere. In 1892 Frere introduced a 'Parish Communion' at 9.30 a.m. on Sundays at St Faith's, Stepney. Frere believed that what was needed in the Church of England was 'a celebration at which it is suitable for the people to communicate, and this must form the chief service of the day'. In his book *Some Principles of Liturgical Reform*, which as we have already seen, was so influential in the period after the publication of the Royal Commission on Ecclesiastical Discipline in 1904, Frere indicated how this might be done.

This is not the place to trace the details of the development of the Liturgical Movement in England, to regret the missed opportunities immediately after the First World War, and the follies leading up to 1927 and 1928; or even to celebrate the contribution of the Sacramental Socialists who added their own particular Anglican dimension to the emerging parish communion. As will be seen, Ronald Jasper chronicled these in great detail in one of his last books. Suffice it to say that the publication in 1935 by A. G. Hebert SSM of *Liturgy and Society* and his editing in 1937 of the book of essays entitled *The Parish Communion*, gave the whole process a tremendous boost.[1]

In the immediate post-war years the movement gained even more pace. A scholarly and beautifully written book by a member of another Anglican religious order, Dom Gregory Dix OSB, appeared as the war ended in 1945; and its scholarship was eagerly taken up both in the Church of England and beyond. In *The Shape of the Liturgy* Dix's important contribution to fresh thinking on the Eucharist was his assertion that the liturgy was constructed not around any pattern of words, but around the four-fold action or 'shape' of taking, blessing, breaking and giving, based on our Lord's own actions at the Last Supper. Later Ronald described it as 'a masterly presentation of the living organism of liturgy. Dix also expressed in moving language the relationship of man to the Eucharist.'[2]

THE SPREAD OF THE PARISH COMMUNION

Gregory Dix's language spoke to those who had now formed what they called 'The Parish and People Movement'. Its founders were Kenneth Packard and Bishop Henry de Candole. The latter became a valued friend and colleague of Ronald's on both the Liturgical Commission and the Joint Liturgical Group. Although not merely concerned with the re-ordering of worship, it was taken for granted that the liturgical base in a 'P & P' parish would be the Parish Communion, probably followed by a Parish Breakfast. In many places a Parish Meeting would be the main weekday activity. In the 1950s, Parish and People was, in many parts of the country, the most active church society. By the nature of things – most meetings were on weekday mornings – it was a heavily clerical affair but its ideas soon influenced every part of parish life. At its meetings priests heard, perhaps for the first time, of the continental (and Roman Catholic) Liturgical Movement. Wartime isolation, combined with the current liturgical conservatism of the Roman Catholic Church in Great Britain, had hidden from the majority of Church of England clergy the important liturgical developments in France, Austria, Germany and Belgium. Now through 'P & P', they learnt about 'dialogue masses', the call for the use of the vernacular, the work of Mont César and Maria Laach; heard for the first time of the writings of Dom Lambert Beauduin, Dom Olivier Rosseau, Louis Bouyer, P.-M. Gy, Josef Jungmann and Bernard Botte.[2]

OPPORTUNITY FOR REFORM

This was a great release for many Anglican 'Catholic' priests who came to realize they need not be imprisoned in the stiff formularies of 'how it ought to be done' according to *Ritual Notes*, or Fortescue, or other Roman or pseudo-Roman ceremonial manuals. They realized that a gap was opening up between their perception of what was liturgically correct, and the developing mind of the Roman Catholic Church. Nevertheless, the fact remained that the majority of clergy were inherently loyal to their ordination promises. Few would have been happy with the attitude of those 'naughty' priests who were alleged to have substituted, 'this and *one* other' (rather than 'this and *none* other') when making the required oaths before ordination. No, the vast majority struggled with what they had been given, but prayed fervently for change. It is a situation which barely forty years later is almost unbelievable and too easily forgotten. Ronald recalled those days:

> While the movement was content to do its best with the eucharistic rite which the Church officially provided, nevertheless the very insights which it proclaimed highlighted the need for some liturgical revision, not least in increased flexibility in rubrical directions and a reconsideration of the structure and content of the eucharistic prayer. Admittedly the movement had its weaknesses – Archbishop Ramsey's criticisms of its views on sacrifice, communion and fellowship received wide publicity; but these were more than offset by its considerable gains. It helped to make the Eucharist the centre of Sunday worship; it engendered peace and unity, breaking down old party differences; and it enabled the congregation to realise itself as the Christian family.[4]

The Church of England was set on the road that would lead eventually to liturgical revision by the work of a very unliturgical Archbishop of Canterbury, Geoffrey Fisher. His biographer Edward Carpenter records:

> When Geoffrey Fisher arrived unexpectedly at Lambeth in 1945 he came to the conclusion that an overriding priority was to restore liturgical order and discipline into the worshipful life of the established Church. Disorder, so he believed, existed to such an extent that it had led to irregularities and confusion in the use of the Book of Common Prayer, much to the irritation of lay worshippers. To quote his own words: 'Because I had the instincts of a headmaster I knew that [coping with this] was absolutely essential for the well-ordering of the Church of England. The lack of order had been quite dreadful.'[5]

THE DECISION TO REFORM CANON LAW

Perhaps Fisher's recent experience in the London diocese coloured his judgement in this matter? Anyway he realized that the task could only really be tackled via a revision of the Canon Law of the Church of England. The archbishops and their advisers believed that if the canons provided for liturgical experimentation, the 1928 situation, in which Church and Parliament found themselves at cross-purposes, need not arise. Services could be tried and tested throughout the church and shown to be acceptable to congregations. Furthermore, the church could be provided with a legal means of adopting services which were not those of the Book of Common Prayer. The programme of Canon Law reform started in the Convocations in 1947, and was not completed until twenty years later. During that time it had engendered a spate of legislation that exceeded anything known in previous English ecclesiastical history. It might seem a brave step for the archbishops to set up, after only eight years of Canon Law debate, a body whose work could only be effective when the necessary legal amendments were in place, but this is what they did.[6]

The first Liturgical Commission, 1955

Archbishop Fisher made it clear from the beginning that the Liturgical Commission's task was to undertake the work which he and the Archbishop of York would decide upon; it was not free to plan its own activities. The Archbishop believed that this limitation would prevent the Commission from being inundated with frivolous requests. A possible request for the production of an Easter Egg Service was Geoffrey Fisher's favourite example of what could happen. From the outset, Ronald saw the potential difficulties in such a restricted remit, being well aware from the work he had so recently completed on Frere's papers, that similar tight controls had frustrated the work of the Advisory Committee on Liturgical Questions between 1912 and 1916. Ronald appealed to Colin Dunlop, the Commission's chairman, to seek a relaxation, but to no avail. Three years later there *were* changes, but not before their inflexibility had already caused difficulties.

The Archbishops' choice of Colin Dunlop as chairman of the Commission was a crucial appointment. The Commission had twenty-one members, and was a fairly academic group with considerable expertise in liturgy and doctrine, but not without a good deal of parochial experience. The various shades of Anglican churchmanship were thought to be fairly represented. That group of lecturers from the 1949 Durham Clergy School were all there, together with such luminaries as Eric Milner-White, E. C. Ratcliff, Kenneth Ross, Mervyn Stockwood, Geoffrey Willis, Cyril Bowles and Eric Abbott. Abbott resigned after twelve months (not having been able to attend even one meeting of the Commission) and was replaced by Arthur Couratin and J. P. Thornton-Duesbury.

That Dunlop had a personal hand in the selection is confirmed in a letter he wrote to Ronald immediately after he had received the Archbishop's invitation to join the Commission. 'I made a special point with the Archbishop that you and one or two others should be asked to serve on the Liturgical Commission and I am very grateful that the Archbishop has concurred. I am very glad that you are pleased.'

CONFLICTING ATTITUDES WITHIN THE COMMISSION

The first meeting of the Commission was held at Lambeth Palace on 12 December 1955. From the beginning, Ronald was fearful about its ability to achieve anything that would be useful. As we have seen, he believed that the *modus operandi* laid down by the archbishops would constrict, if not choke, any really creative liturgical innovations. He knew that the Archbishop was not personally interested in liturgical reform, but was only anxious to have a code of Canon Law which would allow him and the other Bishops to discipline those who strayed beyond its limits. Fisher had not learnt the lesson that G. K. A. Bell had enunciated when commenting on the events of 1927–8: 'The revision of Church services and the enforcement of ecclesiastical discipline are different things. A revision of worship, of common prayer, which is intended from the start to be used as an instrument for stopping disobedience is at any rate not likely to produce the happiest results in the realm of worship!'[7]

Of the Archbishop, Ronald said, 'Where liturgical revision was concerned the Archbishop was really out of his depth: his interest in the subject was minimal and he had no real vision as to the end product.'[8] Nor was he under any illusions about the chairman. True, Dunlop had been one of his initial encouragers in liturgical studies and had insisted to the Archbishop that the otherwise somewhat obscure succentor of Exeter Cathedral would be a benefit to the Commission. But Ronald knew he was a cautious man. This is shown by a letter Dunlop wrote to him in 1952:

> I don't think I agree either with Frere or E. Underhill about frequent changes in the liturgy. This whole idea of 'development' which is so popular nowadays does not arise out of a Christian philosophy at all

> and I cannot see why a liturgy should not be as unchanged as the words of Holy Scripture. A lot was spoken before 1928 of making the new prayer book suit the 'changed needs of modern life' but, as Brightman pointed out, the actual 1928 provisions were really changed due to doctrinal fashions or liturgical fancies and had nothing to do with the 'altered conditions of modern life' at all. I do not object to or wish to advocate, in practice, any changes at all in the P.B. But I think they ought to be very few and very occasional indeed.

Then at the Anglican Congress in Minneapolis in 1954, Dunlop set out his ideas for the criteria to be observed in future liturgical developments in the Anglican Communion. As seen from his 1952 letter he clearly disapproved of alternative forms; he believed they confused the laity and should be kept to the very minimum; and once any new form of service was agreed upon, the old should be scrapped. It therefore followed, Dunlop believed, that any revision should be modest, and should not involve the disappearance of too many familiar landmarks.[9]

With a Chairman who had laid down such criteria only eighteen months beforehand and with the ever-restraining hands of the archbishops hovering over them, it was not surprising that Ronald wondered if there was any likelihood of creative activity by the Commission. Were these the predictable anxieties of a liturgical 'angry young man'? It would have been legitimate to see him in that light. He was not actually the youngest member of Bishop Dunlop's team, that distinction belonged to Bernard Wigan who had been born just twelve months later than Ronald. But at thirty-seven he was a good deal below the average age of the members, which was fifty, and of whom a third had been born in the nineteenth century.

THE COMMISSION'S TASKS

The main tasks for the Commission were outlined to them by the Archbishop. The first was concerned with drawing up a schedule of 'agreed amendments' to the Book of Common Prayer, which could be given immediate statutory authority once the new canon 13 had become law. This canon would be the means by which new forms of services could be authorized and experimentation take place. A second schedule was also to be prepared consisting of more radical variations, mainly from the 1928 book. These would only be for experimental use. Then the Commission was told to look at baptism services with the 'York' rite (a product of the Convocation of York) particularly mentioned. Finally, in preparation for the approaching Lambeth Conference in 1958 the archbishops wanted a survey of the state of liturgical revision throughout the Anglican Communion.

So they started their work. It was decided to commence with Morning and Evening Prayer, and Ronald was deputed to work on the 'intercessions and thanksgivings' with Dr R. V. Sellers, who left his chair in theology at King's London because of eyesight difficulties, and was now a canon of Wells. Within months Canon Sellers was complaining that the work was causing him much toil and that he would need to rest on Ronald's shoulders. This was Ronald's first experience of drafting prayers, and his method and style did not change much in the next twenty-five years. Explaining his work to Dunlop he said: 'As you may realise, Sellers and I do not always agree! Frankly, he rather likes things which are a bit long-winded – redolent with flowery phrases. Personally I prefer simplicity and brevity. Hence, my finished product would tend to be rather more bald than his.'

The style of the revised services – not least the final product, *The Alternative Service Book 1980* – has often been criticized, but we shall see later that Ronald worked hard to find a new and attractive liturgical language for the second half of the twentieth century. The 'thee/thou hump', as Ronald called it, had to be surmounted. He was never certain he had found the right style of liturgical language, no matter how much advice he took from a wide range of poets, scholars and dramatists. One thing he was convinced of was that the style should be neither an imitation nor a pastiche. It would be *sui generis*, and self-authenticating. He believed that an attempt at revision must be made, that a truly incarnational Christianity cannot be stuck in any century, even if the seventeenth century was capable of much linguistic beauty. It was an exploration which fascinated him for the whole of his life. He was both delighted and proud that his son David shared that fascination, with academic distinction, and indeed Ronald and David shared his last book on this very matter.[10] He would not have been surprised to know that the Liturgical Commissions of more recent times have continued the search. Indeed, he would have believed it to be their duty to continue what he began.

In the early days of the Commission there were few supporters of such an attitude even among the members. The secretary (Geoffrey

Willis) wrote to Ronald to say, 'I think you have taken a lot of trouble to provide material for the Commission to select from, but I very much dislike the modern prayers, and now is the chance to say so.' One of the few encouraging letters, among many that were negative like Willis's, is a splendid one from Canon Kenneth Sansbury, one of the Commission, and warden of St Augustine's Canterbury: 'If I may say so, I think you have done an excellent job. You are clearly concerned with the world of 1958 and do not act as some of our brethren do, as though the Holy Spirit ceased to operate in 325 or 1662 or in the days of Bishop Gibson of Gloucester.'

These were not easy days, but Ronald negotiated them with good humour, surviving even a thirty-page handwritten memorandum of comments and criticism from Eric Milner-White. 'A deep apology', writes the Dean, 'that this is in script not type. My Secretary seizes August for her holiday, so I can do no other.'

The Commission produced the report for the Lambeth Conference which the Archbishops had asked for. It was entitled *Prayer Book Revision in the Church of England* and was more conservative and narrowly 'English' in its approach than a similar report from the Indian Church, which regarded a rigid adherence to the standards of 1662 as unacceptable. A flexibility of approach was also emerging in the American Church through its *Prayer Book Studies*. The result was the Lambeth Fathers agreed that 'no Prayer Book, not even that of 1662, can be kept unchanged for ever, as a safeguard of established doctrine'. Ronald was much encouraged by this positive attitude of the Lambeth Fathers. He was moved to compare the Lambeth 1958 recommendations with the Papal Encyclical *Mediator Dei* by means of which, in 1947, Pope Pius XII had put the seal of authority on the Liturgical Movement within the Roman Catholic Church. Of the Lambeth recommendations Ronald wrote: 'They gave a kind of official *imprimatur* to a movement which was already taking place; and they certainly gave useful guidelines to Churches and provinces with only limited expertise at their command.'[11]

Despite this green light, the Church of England's Liturgical Commission did not leap forward in the preparation of new services. True, it still had some time to go before the necessary canons would be in place, and there were many more meetings of the Commission after the publication of the Lambeth Conference report, apparently concerned with small and insignificant matters. Ronald's correspondence of that time is still preoccupied with the minutiae of the intercessions and thanksgiving for Morning and Evening Prayer.

Baptism and Confirmation

Baptism and confirmation were also on the agenda the archbishops had provided. This was proving a painful subject for the Commission. Before the Commission had been formed, the Convocations had themselves tackled the revision of services for baptism and confirmation. From their efforts, emerged a difference of opinion between north and south. What became known as the 'York' rite had many supporters, especially in the northern provinces. At the Commission's third meeting, a decision was taken to make the 'York' rite the basis for an infant service, while redrafting the service for adults. The task of producing this material was given to Arthur Couratin.

Arthur Couratin's arrival on the scene was described by Ronald as 'something of a whirlwind'. Certainly, he soon had his baptism and confirmation draft on the table and it was clear that his recommendations would be more radical than the York proposals. For one thing, they would assume that the administration of baptism and confirmation would normally take place within the Eucharist. There was also a distinct additional emphasis on the role of the Spirit in confirmation and a desire, following Dix, to wrap baptism and confirmation into one rite.

Ronald supported this point of view, and gave Couratin encouragement with this and many other matters over the succeeding years. Their correspondence, of which there is a good deal, is always exceedingly warm and friendly, spiced with humour and the occasional expression of mutual admiration. On a couple of occasions Couratin expresses concern for Ronald's health. 'You looked pale and tired. Don't knock yourself up,' he advised after one meeting. It was very sad that such a fruitful co-operation eventually hit a theological and liturgical disagreement which even their friendship could not surmount, and Couratin felt he had to resign from the Commission.

RECONCILING THE COMMISSION WITH THE CONVOCATIONS

When the drafts for the new services of baptism and confirmation had almost been completed, Ronald thought it was time to raise again his concern about the uncertain relationship between the Commission and the Convocations. The services for baptism and confirmation made for a good example, he believed. Here was work that previously the Convocations had regarded as their own responsibility. What was the status of the drafts now being prepared by an Archbishops' Commission? In particular, who would deal with the task of revising the document in the light of the debates of Convocation? In a memorandum to the Commission he stated:

> This situation is an interesting one and not without its complications, for the Commission has been engaged in a work which hitherto the Convocations have regarded as their own province. From questions which members of the Commission have asked from time to time, it is perfectly clear that, from their point of view at least, there is no clear conception either of the manner in which these rites are to be dealt with by the Convocations, or of their own share – if any – in any subsequent revision of the rites which may be considered necessary. Furthermore, this situation is only the first of a long series of similar situations, for the Commission has been asked to consider the revision of the Book of Common Prayer as a whole. It might therefore be of value to consider very briefly what happened some forty years ago in the case of a former Liturgical Commission, which went by the name of 'The Advisory Committee on Liturgical Questions'.

The memorandum continued with a reminder of the events of 1911–18 and of the way in which 'the Committee of Experts' was marginalized and eventually abandoned by the authorities.

> This first Liturgical Commission failed therefore, not because of the incompetence of its members, but because no satisfactory method was devised for collaboration with the Convocations. It is precisely on this very point – collaboration with the Convocations, that some members of the present Commission feel unhappy. They would feel much happier if the position could be clarified, and they could be assured in some measure that they would not experience the same frustration as their predecessors.[12]

This was not just a young scholar flaunting his unrivalled knowledge of an unhappy aspect of the Church's earlier attempt at liturgical reform; it arose out of a sincere concern for the efficient working of the Commission, so that it might provide the best possible material for the worship of the Church which he served and loved. It was not an issue which was ever fully resolved during Ronald's time with the Commission. The membership of the Commission caused problems from time to time. Had it sufficient liturgical scholars? Were appointments made in order to preserve the churchmanship balance rather than expertise in the subject? Was there too large a component of ecclesiastical politicians who were more anxious to get things through the system than to produce examples of liturgical excellence? Later, after the advent of synodical government in 1970, the Commission became an official board of the General Synod, but even this did not solve all the problems; in fact it created new ones.

It was often observed at the time that Ronald never seemed completely happy when dealing with Convocation, Church Assembly or General Synod; that he was at his most 'headmasterly' on those occasions. Those who have faced those august bodies will know that they are never easy assemblies to address. Furthermore, there are few more difficult subjects than liturgy and the church's worship, with which to face a church audience at any level. Those of us who have undertaken this task at parish, deanery, diocesan or even national level know that everyone present always has their own ideas; everyone believes they know what should be done and what is best, just as well (if not better!) than 'the experts'. There is, in fact, an inbuilt suspicion of liturgical experts. And that is not an entirely unreasonable attitude: worship, rightly understood, is about 'the stuff of life', about basic beliefs and attitudes. It is not an area in which any one of us wants to be disturbed; it is an area in which we certainly 'know what we like' – and too often only 'like what we know'. In a letter to Arthur Couratin, encouraging him to write on liturgy in a Penguin series in 1964 Ronald said:

> This is the one branch of theology which arouses most interest in the man in the street, more than any other – simply because this is where he encounters Christianity at work. A number of people will certainly get hot under the collar about *Honest to God* but it is sheer stupidity to imagine the man in the street does. He gets far more worked up about the changes which might occur in the Parish Communion or Evensong which he has been accustomed to attend. We are desperately in need of creating informed opinion at a popular level about our subject.

At the time when a large amount of liturgical material was passing through the Synod, one cynic observed: 'Having decided we don't trust a group of twenty men and women sitting around a table somewhere or other, to produce our liturgy, we bring together six hundred of us into Church House in Westminster – and do it that way.'

Ronald Jasper was a democrat. He did not subscribe to the view held by Geoffrey Willis, the first secretary of the Commission, who writing to him in March 1962, said he would not be willing to serve on a Commission which is 'tied and bound with instructions not to produce anything worthwhile, but only such silly trifles as the Convocations are likely to accept'. Willis would have reduced the Commission to six members. 'We need a dictatorship as in the sixteenth century,' was his conclusion.

Rather than adopt such an attitude, Ronald was willing to listen to what others thought – witness his constant visiting of colleges, dioceses and conferences of all kinds, particularly during his chairmanship years – although such visits were always bound to produce tremendous frustrations. That he bore them with such patience is a mark of his fortitude and commitment to the task.

Ronald's 1958 memorandum got nowhere; the Commission decided to leave things as they were and continue to work in their previous manner. The *Baptism and Confirmation* report was duly produced, to the obvious dissatisfaction of the Archbishop of Canterbury. 'It was becoming increasingly clear', wrote Ronald, 'that Dr Fisher having asked the Commission to produce something quite new, did not like what we had done.'

Baptism and Confirmation was debated by the convocations in 1960. In the York Convocation it was attacked strongly – first by the lovers of the 'York' rite (including Milner-White) and second by the Archbishop himself. This tone of the Convocation debates produced a crisis of confidence, and the Commission let it be known that the Archbishops must never publish liturgical material and then attack it publicly themselves.

We have already seen that, although Fisher was determined to exercise control over the Commission and its activities, liturgical revision was not a priority with the Archbishop. (Although in retirement he did write a number of long and detailed letters to Ronald about the revision of the Eucharist.) Ronald believed it was the realization that the subject was low on the Archiepiscopal agenda that led to Colin Dunlop's resignation. Ronald recalls that meetings had become a little unruly, with private conversations going on during sessions, of which the chairman (because of increasing deafness) seemed unaware. Ronald was probably looking back on his own time in the chair when he later commented: 'Admittedly the Commission was not an easy body to handle; but a Chairman should be tough and not hesitate to administer rebuke when necessary.'[13]

Those who served under Ronald's chairmanship would recognize the principle of toughness and his abhorrence of cross-table conversation not addressed through the chair to the whole Commission. They would even recall the sharp rap of his pencil (a trait he inherited from his predecessor) to restore order. But they might find it more difficult to recall occasions on which a rebuke was administered – and then only with the utmost courtesy. Ronald's control over meetings had no need of authoritarianism.

NOTES

1. Donald Gray, *Earth and Altar: The Evolution of the Parish Communion in the Church of England to 1945*, Alcuin Club Collections no. 68, Norwich, 1986, *passim.*
2. R. C. D. Jasper, *The Development of the Anglican Liturgy, 1662-1980*, London, 1989 (hereafter *DAL*), p. 179, (see also Simon Bailey, *A Tactful God: Gregory Dix, Priest, Monk, Scholar*, Leominster, 1995, *passim*).
3. John Fenwick and Bryan Spinks, *Worship in Transition, the Twentieth Century Liturgical Movement*, Edinburgh, 1995, pp. 37–52.
4. Jasper, *DAL*, p. 181.
5. Edward Carpenter, *Archbishop Fisher – His Life and Times*, Norwich, 1991, p. 205.
6. Donald Gray, 'The Revision of Canon Law and its Application to Liturgical Revision in the Recent History of the Church of England', *The Jurist*, vol. 48, no. 2, 1988, pp. 638–52.
7. G. K. A. Bell, *Randall Davidson, Archbishop of Canterbury*, 3rd edn, London, 1952, p. 1357.
8. Jasper, *DAL*, p. 212.
9. Jasper, *DAL*, p. 194.
10. R. C. D. Jasper and David Jasper (eds), *Language and the Worship of the Church*, London, 1990.
11. Jasper, *DAL*, p. 217.
12. R. C. D. Jasper, 'Relations between the Commission and the Convocations', *Liturgical Commission Memorandum 13*, n.d. (1958 cf. Jasper, *DAL*, p. 219).
13. Jasper, *DAL*, p. 223.

4

THE COMMISSION'S WORK DEVELOPS

DUNLOP RESIGNED THE chairmanship in September 1960 – although he remained a member of the Commission until its reconstruction two years later. His successor was a very different personality: Donald Coggan, Bishop of Bradford – he of the tapping pencil. Clearly Ronald admired Dr Coggan's handling of the Commission. Describing him as making no claims to be an expert liturgist, he knew that he was an established biblical scholar who was chairing the Commission which eventually produced *The Revised Psalter* in 1963. Coggan continued in office as chairman even after having become Archbishop of York, a fact many believed strengthened the Commission's position in the Church. What certainly made Ronald warm to Donald Coggan was his appreciation of the constitutional questions about which Ronald was so concerned. It was a red letter day for Ronald when on 31 January 1962 *both* Archbishops attended a meeting of the Commission at Lambeth Palace, and announced significant changes in this area.

First of all, there would be closer consultation between the Archbishops and the Commission in formulating policy, so that the latter would know more precisely what was required of it. Relations with the House of Bishops would be improved by discussing proposals with them before they went to the Convocations. Second, the Commission would have a broader base, with both male and female lay representation.

There was one more meeting of the existing Commission in March 1962, to complete the revision of Morning and Evening Prayer and the associated material (not least the ubiquitous thanksgivings and intercessions). The result was 'a very conservative report with not a tremendous lot to show for over seven years' work,' Ronald observed.

The new Commission, with Bishop Coggan in the chair met for the first time in September 1962 and had considerable changes in its membership. Half of the original members had disappeared. It did not take them long to decide that the top priority should be the revision of the Eucharist. Things seemed to be moving at last, and if only the necessary legislation could be got into place there could be real progress. The draft canon 13 (on liturgical revision) had by this time been divided into five parts – consequently they were now known as 'canons B 1–5. To save time, the legislation giving effect to these canons – the Prayer Book (Alternative and other Services) Measure – was drafted and introduced into the Church Assembly even while the canons were being considered. This legislative process in fact came to a successful conclusion in the House of Commons on 23 March 1965 with the Measure coming into effect on 1 May the following year. But before 1966 a good deal of work needed to be accomplished, and the Archbishop of Canterbury attended the Commission meeting in April 1964 to make this point.

During those days, Ronald travelled up from Exeter to the Commission and other meetings. Exeter provided a pleasant and congenial place in which to work, and life in and around the Cathedral supplied an agreeable spiritual and liturgical background against which Ronald's other work could develop. But as the work on the Headlam biography began to near completion and the demands of the Liturgical Commission grew, so did thoughts of a new job.

The move to King's

King's College London had a long tradition of teaching liturgy. The list of liturgy lecturers is impressive: C. F. Rogers, Oscar Hardman, E. C. Ratcliff, F. E. Croydon. It even reached back to Percy Dearmer, that enigmatic figure of the turn of the century whose *The Parson's Handbook* exceeded the sales of any other book on liturgy for many years. King's and its traditions were by this time well known to Ronald through his Headlam studies. The post at King's became vacant when Benedict Green, who had combined the task with that of sub-warden of the Theological Hostel in Vincent Square, went to test his vocation with the Community of the Resurrection.

Sydney Evans, the Dean of King's, approached Ronald about the post in the summer of 1959. Bishop Hannay cautioned him to consider whether, because of the demands of university administration, he would have enough leisure at King's to pursue his other work, and supplied an anecdote and some advice: 'Henry Chadwick told me that he met C. H. Dodd after his resignation of his chair had been announced, and said how much he regretted it. Dodd replied, "My dear Chadwick I shall now be able to do some work." Not helpful I fear. But at any rate I will "pit up a wee bit prayer" that you may see the Lord's way plain before your face, so that you may do the best service to Him and to His Church.' On being told more details of the job, his old episcopal friend said, 'I congratulate you on your KCL appointment and wish you all joy of it. I am so glad you will have a job calculated to use the powers the good Lord has given you.' Ronald decided to accept the post; he moved his family to Dulwich in the summer of 1960 and commenced lecturing at King's at the beginning of the Michaelmas term.

Additionally, London would allow him to develop another of his new interests – the Alcuin Club. He had joined the committee in 1957. The club had published his Frere correspondence as one of their 'Collections' in 1954.[1] The Alcuin Club Collections are a series of books on liturgical subjects which began in 1899 (and to which Frere contributed nine volumes). The Alcuin Club was formed in 1897 to promote liturgical studies by publishing books and pamphlets. It performed a notable service to the Church in the period running up to the 1927 Prayer Book revision proposals, through its publications on liturgical reform. Their distinctive orange paper covers distinguished their scholarly Catholic position from the Green Book of the more avowedly Anglo-Catholic Church Union and the modernist Grey Books.

Just before his arrival in London, the Alcuin Club had published in their more modest 'Pamphlet' series a monograph by Ronald – *The Position of the Celebrant at the Eucharist.*[2] In his first academic year at King's he delivered a paper to the annual meeting of the Alcuin Club, which was subsequently published in the same pamphlet series. In that lecture he surveyed the work of British scholars on the origins of the eucharistic liturgy. Entitled *The Search for an Apostolic Liturgy*, the paper combined the work that he was now doing in his lectures at King's with the researches which he knew were needed to inform any part he might have in the Liturgical Commission's new task of preparing a revision of the eucharistic liturgy.[3]

The offer of the chairmanship

It was new tasks such as these now being laid upon the Commission, and not least the burden of having to pilot them through the Convocations and the Assembly, that convinced Archbishop Coggan that it was time to give up the chairmanship of the Commission. As we have seen, he continued in the post when he left Bradford for the primacy at York, and there was no doubt that having an archbishop presiding had lifted the profile of the Commission. But during the next stage, which would involve a good deal of legislative business, it might not be tactically advantageous to have one of the Primates presenting the material.

The choice of Ronald was a surprise for many. He had been one of the youngest members of the Commission when it was first appointed in 1955, and there were still many on the Commission who could be described as senior both in age and appointment. More surprised, even than them, was Ronald himself. For his reaction we can do no better than turn to one of the most fascinating autobiographical passages in *The Development of the Anglican Liturgy*. He writes of his meeting with Dr Coggan in the Athenaeum on Wednesday 25 September 1964 when he told Ronald of the Primates' proposal. 'He and the Archbishop of Canterbury were keen that I should take over, and if possible straight away. This was quite unexpected; and I remember temporizing by asking how long I would be expected to cope. He replied, "Until the whole job is done." But I think neither of us then realised that this would take over sixteen years, bringing me almost to the end of my active working life.'[4]

Ronald's feelings were mixed. He was gratified to be asked but he was not sure whether it was what he wanted to do at that precise moment. He realized that the job would make considerable demands upon his time and energy, and he had to decide whether it was the direction in which he wanted his life to go: 'I enjoyed working with the Commission; but I was wedded to university teaching, and I had almost finished the biography of Bishop Bell with other possibilities of a great deal more writing already in the offing. I was, in fact, doing the very things in life I had always wanted to do; and to take on the Commission would not only involve a serious disruption, it would also mean an end to further writing for a very long time.'[5]

In this his prognostications were absolutely correct. After Bell, he was never able to undertake another ecclesiastical biography. The only exception was a short life of H. N. Bate.[6] Among his friends, he often expressed regret about this, and hoped that at least retirement might provide the opportunity. It did not. It gave us his invaluable *The Development of the Anglican Liturgy* with those fascinating passages of autobiography, but he was never able to return to his first love, writing the lives of twentieth-century churchmen.

Then there was another minus. We have already commented on Ronald's demeanour in Convocation and Synod, and it would seem that his aversion to such assemblies was fundamental: 'Nor could I raise any enthusiasm at the prospect of being involved with the Convocations and the Church Assembly, a world I had hitherto studiously avoided. One part of me there protested violently, and my first inclination was to say "No".'[7]

As he pondered these things, Ronald realized there were also very good reasons why he should accept. He already had a good relationship with the Archbishop of York; in fact, the latter made it clear from the start that he had personally recommended Ronald. Dr Coggan also told the present writer that he had no hesitation in recommending Ronald to his fellow Archbishop. Having worked alongside him on the Commission for four years, Coggan had first-hand evidence of Ronald's capability. Privately, Ronald thought he knew of one reason for his selection. He twice told Colin Buchanan that at a meeting during the period of Donald Coggan's chairmanship, Ronald had boiled over at some internal opposition and had told two gentlemen not to be obstructive idiots – to the Archbishop's visible pleasure. The task of convincing the Archbishop of Canterbury of his suitability would have been something like pushing on an open door. Geoffrey Fisher had retired from Canterbury in 1961 and had been succeeded by a long-time admirer of Ronald – Michael Ramsey. The new Archbishop had, as we have seen, taken a keen interest in Ronald's career both when Dr Ramsey was a Professor at Durham, and again when he returned there as bishop. 'There were strong ties of both respect and friendship, particularly with Michael Ramsey. We had known each other for some twenty-five years and in my Durham days I owed him an enormous debt, with help and encouragement in a variety of ways. I knew I could get on with him and I was not afraid to argue or disagree with him.'[8]

A few days later, both Archbishops wrote to Ronald. The Archbishop of York hoped that he had not given him too much of a shock, while the Archbishop of Canterbury told him how 'glad and grateful I am for your readiness to take on the chairmanship'. The die was cast.

No time was lost, and the news was conveyed to the Commission just a few days later on 30 September, by Dr Coggan. Ronald commented: 'I think most of them were surprised . . . but on the whole they took it very well.'

NOTES

1. R. C. D. Jasper (ed.) *Walter Howard Frere: His Correspondence on Liturgical Revision and Construction*, Alcuin Club Collections no. XXXIX, London, 1954.
2. R. C. D. Jasper, *The Position of the Celebrant at the Eucharist*, Alcuin Club Pamphlet no. XVI, London, 1959.
3. R. C. D. Jasper, *The Search for an Apostolic Liturgy*, Alcuin Club Pamphlet no. XVIII, London, 1963.
4. R. C. D. Jasper, *The Development of the Anglican Liturgy, 1662–1980*, (hereafter *DAL*), London, 1989, p. 240.
5. Jasper, *DAL*, p.240.
6. Ronald Jasper, *Herbert Newall Bate: A Reticent Genius*, York, 1987.
7. Jasper, *DAL*, p. 240.
8. Jasper, *DAL*, p. 240.

5

CHAIRMAN OF THE LITURGICAL COMMISSION

THE NEW CHAIRMAN was keen to stamp his own authority on the work of the Commission. He believed that the best way forward would be by means of a three-fold plan. The first principle in such a plan would be to cease tinkering with the 1662 liturgy – devotees should be allowed to continue to use it as it was and always had been. The second need was for some kind of 'sales exercise' and thirdly he wanted to commend the principle of 'live and let live'.

It seemed to Ronald that to put to death '1662' by some legal fiat would be both unkind and unnecessary. What was needed he believed, was a series of alternative services to place alongside the Book of Common Prayer, rather than to replace it.

Principles applied

That this was his basic principle was widely ignored by the developing band of Prayer Book fundamentalists who saw Ronald Jasper as their chief bogey-man. He was a great lover of the Prayer Book; in one of his last writings he described Thomas Cranmer as 'the great master'. Yet he was seized by the necessity to produce a liturgy which was in a dignified form, used the language of the twentieth century, and had learnt from the historical researches of the centuries since 1662. His opponents' lack of a historical perspective saddened Ronald. It was a fact that 1662 had always had its critics; his first book had clearly demonstrated that. His second had described the efforts, eventually frustrated, to take notice of the situation which the 1904 Royal Commission had identified, namely that 'the law of public worship in the Church of England is too narrow for the religious life of the present generation'. More significantly, it was still the case, just as it had been in 1904, that the specific legal prohibition on any variation from the Book of Common Prayer 'needlessly condemns much which a great section of Church people, including many of her most devoted members value'.[1]

It was for such a raft of reasons that Ronald Jasper and his colleagues on the Liturgical Commission undertook the long and detailed work of liturgical revision. They worked for the folk who were needlessly condemned; for the sake of historical and liturgical integrity; and to provide a vehicle by means of which a local congregation could praise, thank and worship Almighty God in a way, and in a language, which they would feel was authentic for them and their neighbours.

No one, least of all Ronald, had any illusions. Liturgical revision was not going to bring about the conversion of England. Often, the new services were condemned because they failed to fill the churches and bring back the young people 'as you said they would do' (many a correspondent claimed). No such claims were ever made at any time for the programme of liturgical reform; those involved were not so idiotic. Rather was it true that in his sixteen years of leadership, Ronald attempted to supply the Church with something which it had been seeking for many years. That it did not please or satisfy everyone was not in the least surprising. As we have said, we are dealing with 'the stuff of life'.

The chairman's workload

The second principle that Ronald realized must govern his work with the Commission was what he described as 'some sort of sales exercise'. His own experience and knowledge of parish life made him sensitive to the need for the Commission to create a caring image; infecting people with its own convictions and enthusiasms, convincing them that it was not a body of high and dry academics living up in the clouds, but a group of sensitive people, concerned with the spiritual welfare of others. A good deal could be achieved with the pen, that he knew; but it was perhaps more important that individual members of the Commission should be ready to go out and talk to people 'and it was incumbent upon me to set a good example'.

In the next decade, Ronald visited every diocese in both provinces. He also made it a golden rule that no letter or enquiry should ever be left unanswered. His biographer, who has had to cope with thirty boxes of correspondence (containing no less than 10,000 letters) can vouch that the 'golden rule' was applied religiously. The letters are of infinite variety and, not unexpectedly, many are unpleasant. Ronald wrote that even though he expected some adverse correspondence, he was surprised by the tone and content of some of the letters and commented, 'I did not expect "fan mail" from people who deliberately set out to be vindictive or offensive; it was incredible how cruel some so-called Christians could be.' But only occasionally, and then only to a few, did he admit to being both shocked and hurt by some of those letters.

If a year is chosen from the time during which he was chairman, one which was not particularly frenetic or concentrated, it is possible to assess the work that was involved over and above his normal clerical duties. Take, for example, 1970. By then, Series Two Holy Communion had been in use for a couple of years, and the results of a questionnaire on its acceptability had been published, with 77 per cent of those replying wishing to continue using the rite (a figure which went up to 90 per cent as far as the clergy were concerned). *Common Prayer 1970*, a revision of Morning and Evening Prayer, had been presented to the Convocations, and the General Synod had been inaugurated by the Queen. During that year, Ronald received 476 letters on Commission business to which he applied his 'golden rule'. A significant proportion of the letters were from members of the Commission, often attaching long schedules of liturgical material. Each of those received equally long and equally detailed replies. Others were from bishops asking for help, Religious Orders seeking assistance over the revision of their Divine Office (there were seven of these in progress at one time during the year), and with letters from cathedrals, universities, and ordinary men and women in the pew.

Letters also came from all over the world. That year from: South Africa, India, Iran, Vietnam, Australia, Belgium, France, Sweden, Israel and a great many from the United States. Predictably, there was a constant stream from both Bishopsthorpe and Lambeth. From the latter came requests for aid and advice such as: how (or can) you deconsecrate a church? do you need to be made deacon before you are ordained priest? should lay-folk and clergy join bishops in the laying on of hands at episcopal consecrations?

Alongside such letters come the many requests for a talk, lecture or sermon. Among the letters that Ronald wrote that year there is no example of a refused invitation. Diaries are frequently adjusted so that a mutually convenient date can be found. The result is that Newcastle is reached by using the overnight sleeper, allowing an extra talk to be fitted into a hectic three days in the diocese at Hexham, Alnwick and Newcastle itself. This was a diocesan occasion, as were visits to Coventry and Lichfield, but invitations to rural deaneries would not be declined. Nor did the chairman of the Commission ever stand on his dignity; he would willingly address parish groups in Hove, Shrewsbury, Sherborne, Plymouth and Epsom, for example. Then there were the religious communities (the Sisters at Fairacres and West Malling, say) and theological colleges of all churchmanship (Ridley and St Chad's, Durham). One particular invitation which gave him great personal pleasure was to be asked to speak to the General Chapter of the Community of the Resurrection at Mirfield. Our list for 1970 has still not included the RAF chaplains, cathedral precentors, the Fellowship of Catholic Priests in Oxford, the West Surrey Clerical Association and the Readers of Guernsey. They all received his individual attention and, to judge from their letters of thanks, very much appreciated having heard from the fount of wisdom itself. It was an impressive undertaking, and more than fulfilled his objective for the Commission of 'explaining and commending' and infecting with their own 'convictions and enthusiasms'. And that was only one year!

This was also the year in which he undertook an extensive tour of the United States, visiting among other places the seminaries at Seabury Weston, Cambridge, Mass., both General and Union in New York and the World Center for Liturgical Studies in Florida. He preached at Harvard and in St John the Divine Cathedral, New York. One of the prime organizers of this trip was Dr Edgar Brown, the director of the Lutheran Commission on Worship, who was his host six years later when Susquehanna University conferred the degree of Doctor of Letters, *honoris causa* on him.

Role of the arts in the new liturgy

As chairman, Ronald was aware of the need for attractive literature to complement the verbal presentation and encouraged others to provide it, knowing that it was not his personal forte. Filmstrips, films, and later videos were produced to give visual stimulation to the work. A group who had experience in religious drama was brought together to work on the presentation of various aspects of the liturgy, and there was also a group with expertise in architecture and the visual arts who worked on the setting for worship and also such matters as vesture. Ronald was one of the earliest advocates in the Church of England of the now universally popular cassock-alb. He kept close contact with musicians. Lionel Dakers, his friend from Exeter days, was a regular adviser, as was Alan Wicks at Canterbury. Regular visits to Addington Palace kept the Royal School of Church Music (RSCM) informed about the progress of revision, and the commissioning of John Rutter, then a still mainly unknown composer, to write a setting for Series Three Holy Communion, was a result of Ronald's own enthusiasm. Rutter's setting of the Eucharist was first sung at a service for the Commission in the chapel of Church House, Westminster in the presence of the composer. All this illustrated Ronald's firmly held conviction that good liturgy does not just depend upon the right words and texts; but it is an entire offering of body, mind and spirit, involving all our senses and drawing upon the best that human ingenuity can devise, in order that we might present an offering which is worthy of the God whom we worship.

The third of the principles which he had enunciated, certainly generated more writing, debating and persuading than any other aspect of the chairman's role. Ronald was determined to commend the principle of 'live and let live'. The phrase, in this context, seems to have originated with Arthur Couratin and is taken up regularly in the frequent letters which passed between him and Ronald. The phrase was an attempt to express the principle that the Church of England is a comprehensive church. Since 1662, whenever that principle had been ignored, the Church had clearly suffered. Ronald believed that services needed to be expressed in sufficiently broad terms to command general acceptance. Couratin spelt this out in 1965 in a letter he wrote to Basil Naylor, and which Ronald felt important enough to copy, keep and file. 'I am worried because I suspect that some people want to produce liturgical forms which will enable them, not only to express what they themselves believe, but also exclude what they do not approve of other people believing. In correspondence with the Archbishop of York the phrase "Live and let live" has been used and approved; and this principle has, I hope, governed all my drafting.'

When, sadly, Couratin resigned from the Commission over the *anamnesis* in the Series Two Eucharistic Prayer, he believed that this principle had been abandoned; whereas Ronald was of the opinion that the compromise he had achieved in this matter was still within the realms of general acceptability. Obtaining the right balance in matters concerning the Eucharistic Prayer, with which both Catholic and Evangelical felt comfortable, was one of two matters which recur over and over again in Ronald's correspondence and which, Ronald believed, could be tackled according to this principle. The other was the matter of prayers for the departed.

Evangelical participants

A distinct change came over the Church of England during the time Ronald was concerned with the revision of its liturgy. The revision eventually took place against a background which was, in one particular respect, basically different to that which he had carefully and accurately chronicled through his editorship of the Frere Papers. In the pre-1928 period there were, as we saw earlier, three proposals for revision on the table for the Convocations to consider as they formulated their own proposals. Two of the liturgical 'position papers' came from the Catholic end of the Church, the Church Union and the Alcuin Club, while the third came from the more (theologically) liberal 'Life and Liberty' movement. No textual contribution to the debate came from the Evangelicals. Their voice, while not unheard, was essentially negative, committed to the rejection of the Revised Prayer Book and more than content with the *status quo*. However, by the time the first Liturgical Commission was appointed in 1955, things had changed among Evangelicals, particularly with regard to the revision of the Eucharist. As Christopher Cocksworth has pointed out in his *Evangelical eucharistic thought in the Church of England*, 'Evangelicals began to admit that their recent theological approaches towards the Eucharist had been unnecessarily defensive and therefore had tended towards a false reductionalism. Evangelicals began to draw on the more positive aspects of their tradition, experiment with new ideas and enter into a tentative dialogue with Catholic emphases.'[2]

This change in attitude was only marginally reflected in the composition of the original Commission. Evangelicals were included (such as Douglas Harrison, Cyril Bowles, Douglas Horsfield) but the more conservative wing of that party did not believe that such men fully represented their views. Even after the 1962 reconstitution of the Commission they were not altogether happy with the Evangelical 'team' of Donald Coggan, Douglas Harrison, F. J. Taylor and Cyril Bowles. Their anxiety was heightened, because at about that time there was a growing realization among some Evangelicals that their position would be unrepresented during the revision process; and that, consequently, they would once again be forced to adopt a negative attitude – and this they did not wish to happen. Cocksworth again:

> Evangelicals had a great love for the 1662 communion service. They saw it as essentially Cranmer's rite. They had profound respect for his skill in devising a liturgy of great beauty which was profoundly devotional and an apt expression of Reformed doctrine. However, despite this admiration there was, on the one hand, an increasing recognition of the inevitability of liturgical revision and, on the other, an acceptance that at many points it could be improved and that a more modern form was necessary.[3]

With these considerable responsibilities on his sufficiently broad shoulders, the conservative-evangelicals' liturgical hero – Colin O. Buchanan – entered the scene in September 1964.

A scholar of considerable energy and enthusiasm, Colin Buchanan quickly brought to the Commission a point of view hitherto unrepresented and, by his personal efforts, brought about a sea-change among those of his theological persuasion. His entry on to the liturgical scene also coincided with a considerable increase in the number of evangelical ordinands – in the first place probably as a result of the Billy Graham evangelistic campaigns – and the resulting rise in confidence of the Evangelical party within the Church of England over the years. Colin also kept alongside the growing Charismatic Movement and laboured to maintain a two-way channel for liturgical concerns among those influenced by that movement. Ronald must have been somewhat nervous of the way in which Colin would fit into the Commission.

Ronald recalls his arrival: 'He came with a reputation of being a very able scholar of decidedly Conservative Evangelical views: and at first he was clearly conscious of his position as a rather lonely representative of a particular party line. But it did not take him long to lose his nervousness or whatever prickles he may have had; and we all came to appreciate his cheery and uncompromising presence.'[4]

Ronald admitted that at the outset, Colin Buchanan's stand on things such as prayers for the departed and the Eucharistic Prayer, undoubtedly created problems. Yet they were, they both believed, problems capable of ultimate resolution; and Ronald was never less than appreciative of his contribution. He wrote of Colin, 'Over the years he gave a great deal to the Commission.'[5]

In 1964 Arthur Couratin was responsible for the drafting of proposals for the Eucharist (what was to be known as Series Two) and he was anxious to have an early meeting with Colin Buchanan. Couratin wrote to Ronald, 'Colin Buchanan lunches with me on Monday. I will try him out on "live and let live". But I don't think I will get very far.' Couratin, and others of his way of thinking, found that although Evangelicals were willing to 'live and let live' to a certain extent, there was now a large evangelical constituency which was anxious to have a revision of the Eucharist which they all could use. They would not be satisfied with being told that they could always use the Book of Common Prayer; the Evangelicals were keen to have something modern and up-to-date, but acceptable to their point of view.

Ronald came to appreciate this point of view; and after the death of E. C. Ratcliff in 1967, and the resignation of Arthur Couratin and the appointment of a new Commission in 1968 in which there was an attempt to strengthen the evangelical representation, he expended a good deal of time and effort in trying to find a way through the controversies. In particular, the problem of framing a Eucharistic Prayer which would be acceptable to everyone in the Church of England was a personal concern. The result was that the General Synod eventually produced a eucharistic rite for inclusion in the Alternative Service Book, which even such contrasting die-hards as Brian Brindley and Roger Beckwith could commend. Although he did not take part in this particular piece of horse-trading (which took place at the Revision Committee stage of Synodical proceedings), the fact that it was able to take place at all can be credited to the change of attitude which Ronald had engendered. It was a stance which had moved beyond one of 'live and let live' to one of 'we all need to live together'. It may have been a stance which those who belonged to the Anglo-Catholic end of the Church (from which he himself derived) found hardest to accept; but it was in the interest of the peace of the Church for the time being. No one, not least Ronald, would be surprised to know that the debate on the eucharistic offering still goes on. Perhaps it is one of those matters which will only be settled at the end of all things.

NOTES

1. *Report of the Royal Commission on Ecclesiastical Discipline*, (cd 3040), 1906, para 399, p. 75.
2. Christopher Cocksworth, *Evangelical eucharistic thought in the Church of England*, Cambridge, 1993, p. 97.
3. Cocksworth, *Evangelical Eucharistic Thought*, p. 110.
4. Jasper, *DAL*, p. 241.
5. Jasper, *DAL*, p. 241.

6

ECUMENICAL LITURGICAL WORK

UNTIL THE 1960s, the Liturgical Movement in the Roman Catholic Church, the Parish and People movement in the Church of England, the Church Service Society in the Church of Scotland, the Methodist Sacramental Fellowship, and other stirrings in the protestant churches in Scandinavia, the United States, Canada and elsewhere, were seeds growing secretly – and independently – within their own churches. True, the leaders of these organizations usually knew of each others' work, but there was little awareness in the Church as a whole of the fact that a great change was coming over the worship of the western church, that participation and accessibility were the order of the day, and that all churches were agreed about the centrality of the Eucharist in Christian worship.[1]

The Faith and Order movement was one of the first points of exchange. After the Edinburgh conference in 1937, one of the international commissions it appointed was asked to prepare a report on *Ways of Worship*. The 1939–45 war inevitably slowed the process of its preparation considerably, but it was published in time for the Lund Conference of Faith and Order in 1952. This was a descriptive book: what the various churches themselves believed about their worship – it contained no call for liturgical co-operation.[2]

In his own lifetime, Ronald remained under-recognized for his pioneering role in the area of ecumenical liturgical co-operation. In the Church of England, this area was often – and perhaps still is – viewed with considerable suspicion. The General Synod was usually unwilling to accept the recommendations of ecumenical bodies without considerable questioning; and the fact that the Alternative Service Book eventually contained so many ecumenical elements is entirely due to Ronald's perseverance over a matter to which he was deeply committed.

The move from Exeter to King's London, was the catalyst, Ronald explained. He found that within London University he was not just teaching Anglicans, and that he came into contact with clergy and scholars from other churches who had similar interests. For instance at Richmond College, a Methodist establishment, he came to know Marcus Ward who had been involved in the creation of the South-India rite; Norman Goldhawk, a hymnologist; and later Raymond George, who was to be a companion and colleague in many ecumenical liturgical adventures. From New College he was in contact with Congregationalists like John Huxtable and Geoffrey Nuttall; while from mainly student contacts he came to know the Baptists Neville Clark and Stephen Winward. However, it is to a Church of Scotland scholar that Ronald pays particular tribute as an initial inspirer, and to a paper read to the Edinburgh Theological Society by Dr John Lamb in March 1960. This was published in *The Annual of the Church Service Society* later that year, and was to be of significance for the newly arrived liturgy lecturer at King's. He wrote of the article that it 'first suggested to me that talking together about liturgy was not enough: creating liturgy together would be more productive: and he [Lamb] firmly believed that this offered more opportunity for progress towards Christian unity than any other activity.'[3]

The Joint Liturgical Group

The suggestion that there might be some kind of co-operation in the field of liturgy was first mooted by Ronald in a conversation with Donald Coggan in December 1960. He pleaded that it was high time for the possibilities of an interdenominational exercise, despite all the difficulties, to be explored. During the next year or so, he continued to try out the idea on individuals and small groups. He did not always get support. Geoffrey Willis, secretary of the Liturgical Commission, poured typically very cold (and Church of England) water on the suggestion: 'I do not think that your suggestion of co-operation with outsiders is at all practical. A seminar such as this might be useful as an informal affair for the exchange of views among scholars, but as a practical proposition it is quite unworkable. You know that it is bad enough to get a pure C of E body to agree on anything: how much more impossible to secure agreement if you broaden the theological and doctrinal basis still further.' In the face of such clear opposition, it needs a real commitment to a principle to persevere. Ronald had that. It is important to keep in mind that these convictions were held by one who, at the time, was just an ordinary member of the Commission. There was no special reason why he should be listened to by the church authorities. Early in 1962 Ronald returned to the matter in a letter to the Archbishop of York, the chairman of the Liturgical Commission (Donald Coggan), to which he had a more encouraging reply: 'I see the importance . . . but I am wondering what you think would be the best way forward. Do you feel that we ought to have a non-Anglican liturgical expert serving regularly on the Commission, or do you think . . . that your point would best be met by a sub- committee which co-opts liturgical scholars of persuasions other than the Anglican?'

In a long response, dated 18 March 1962, Ronald thanks the archbishop for the encouragement he has given him by not dismissing his suggestion out of hand. He says that he realizes that his idea will be anathema to many members of the Commission, but he goes on, 'I've always felt that one of our weaknesses in the past has been our failure to face realities: too often we have become a liturgical seminar, pure and simple: and the lessons of the past have been ignored – to our cost.' He then made the point that if worship is the fundamental work and function of the Church, we ought to recognize the fact in our ecumenical work – or at least to recognize the principle.

Ronald also tells the Archbishop that he realizes that there are no precedents for what he proposes, 'so we can only feel our way and proceed by means of trial and error'. The idea of observers does not appeal; he wants a small body of two, three or four to investigate the possibility, but he literally underlines that they must be *officially appointed.* It must be formal or official, rather than informal. 'Informal work just gets forgotten. History can give us scores of instances of this. Only in the rarest of cases does the work of private individuals receive serious attention.' As he wrote this, could he have been thinking again of Bishop Frere, who took part in the abortive 'Malines Conversations' between 1921 and 1935? Frere's papers in the Borthwick Library in York contain, as well as the ten boxes on liturgy on which Ronald worked, five boxes of correspondence and papers on that brave attempt to find some means of reconciliation between the Papacy and the Anglican Church. But the Conversations were always unofficial and received no token of approval from either side, and so could be allowed to 'wither on the branch'.[4] Malines would engage Ronald's attention later on in his ministry at York.

As his letter to the archbishop continues, Ronald warms to his subject. He argues that ecumenical co-operation would enable those involved to achieve a valuable insight into worship as a whole – comparative liturgy. 'Time, labour and energy might well be saved if only we would all stop doing our work in splendid isolation. To put it at its very crudest, if we worried a little more about what Scotland is actually doing and a little less about what we think Hippolytus did, we might get somewhere. If needs be, we can study Hippolytus together.' This remarkable letter ends with a rare personal revelation. Ronald feels confident enough in his relationship with Donald Coggan to lift for once a corner of his personal reserve. 'I don't want to appear a prig or a prophet, but my explorations of the modern liturgical and ecumenical fields have been in some ways unique: and long ago these experiences impelled me to plead two points in the Commission's work – the Convocations and relations with the public. On both points I was beaten: but bitter experience has justified both pleas. I feel equally sure now that if we sleep in on this point of co-operation, we shall throw away something of tremendous value.'

Just a year later, Ronald was specifically encouraged to convene a two-day meeting during the Easter vacation at King's College Hostel in Vincent Square, to which a dozen handpicked Baptists, Congregationalists, Methodists, Presbyterians and Anglican liturgical scholars from England and Scotland were invited. Most were there with the full knowledge and consent of their own church authorities. John Huxtable expressed the feelings of them all when he said, 'This is what we have been waiting for.' By the end of the second day it was agreed that a Joint Liturgical Group (JLG) should be formed, and that the Archbishop of Canterbury should be asked to help to bring it into being. Ronald reported this to the Archbishop of York who in turn told Lambeth. The result was that Ronald had a letter from Michael Ramsey which was somewhat cautious, but in which the archbishop said he was willing to talk to him on the subject. They met and Ronald's arguments must have been persuasive, because the Archbishop of Canterbury agreed to issue invitations to an inaugural meeting of the Joint Liturgical Group in October 1963.

At this meeting Douglas Harrison, the Dean of Bristol, was elected chairman, and Ronald as secretary – a position which he held until his retirement from the Group in 1980. The work of the JLG in the next seventeen years, during which Ronald edited and contributed to all of the nine publications the Group produced in that time, proved to be a source of enormous personal satisfaction. Looking back just twelve months before his death, he spoke of the Group's work and his part in it with a warmth that never particularly permeated his remarks about the Church of England Commission. It was *his* creation, it was the first such body in the world – the important North American Consultation on Common Texts was not formed until 1964 – and its work blazed a trail which others followed. Ronald was rightly proud that he refused to be discouraged, and that it justified his persistence. 'I must confess that working with this Group was exhilarating: members were keen and worked tremendously hard; there were no ecclesiastical politics to bother about; and members were stimulated by the fresh insights which the representatives of other Churches provided. We were all conscious of the lack of any Roman Catholic contribution; but this was remedied before very long.'

Roman Catholic Liturgical evolutions.

The invitations to join the JLG had all been to non-Roman Churches. This was seen as realistic back in 1963, before the effects of the Second Vatican Council became felt in the realms of liturgical co-operation. Such hesitations, it would seem, were not in Ronald's mind. In January 1964 he approached the Archbishop of York once again; this time to explore the possibility of some closer work with Rome. He had been talking to Anglican theologian Eric Mascall, who told him that he had close connections among Roman Catholics, and knew they were considering what might be done about liturgical forms for English Roman Catholics, now that Vatican II had decided that Mass could be said in the vernacular.

Mascall believed that Roman Catholics were anxious 'to keep in step with a number of things which other people do in this country'. Did the Archbishop think, Ronald asked, that he would be cutting across anyone else's territory if he were to talk with Bishop Gordon Wheeler, Roman Catholic Bishop of Leeds, and Eric Mascall and discuss 'unofficially (and *very* tactfully) the lie of the land?' It is interesting that when the subject of Roman Catholics came up, Ronald was at first willing to modify his earlier stated antagonism to 'unofficial talks'. No doubt he was right to tread carefully at this stage.

TESTING ANGLICAN–ROMAN LITURGICAL CO-OPERATION

Donald Coggan gave the go-ahead. 'I do not see', he replied, 'why, on a purely personal basis and quite unofficially, you should not confer with Gordon Wheeler and Eric Mascall.' The Archbishop thought that 'there was everything to be gained by keeping in touch with our Roman brethren on matters liturgical'. This proved to be a piece of encouragement which was destined to bear fruit. In the event, probably because they were now both working in Yorkshire, Bishop Henry de Candole of Knaresborough (a member of the Liturgical Commission and also a Church of England representative on JLG) met with Bishop Wheeler in July 1964. Bishop de Candole wrote to Ronald: 'I lunched yesterday with Gordon Wheeler who was *most* friendly and welcoming. He discussed, from his side, their problems of Englishing the Liturgy. This is obviously a matter on which *we* and *they* ought to be in contact (a) in regard to 'common forms' – Creed, Gloria etc. and (b) in regards to the principles of the use of English in worship today. I can't see (and he can't either) why we should not counsel together on this whole matter.' Bishop de Candole also reports that Roman Catholics would be interested to know about the work of the Joint Liturgical Group.

From the winter of 1964, in his new position as chairman of the Commission, Ronald was able to move forward rapidly the matter of co-operation with Roman Catholics. At his first meeting in the chair, he invited two lay Roman Catholics who were members of the newly-formed Liturgical Translation Committee for the RC Church in England: Bernard Dunne, the liturgical director of Burns and Oates, and Professor Herbert Finberg. Professor Finberg, from the University of Leicester, had been co-translator of what was known as the Knox Missal (because it used the biblical translation of Ronald Knox). He had long been an advocate of the vernacular in the liturgy. The following April, Ronald asked the Archbishop of Canterbury if he could open up this whole matter of agreed English texts with both the Roman Catholics and the Free Churches. 'The time is ripe,' he informs Dr Ramsey, 'Professor Finberg, who is largely responsible for the Englishing of the Roman texts, did tell us that he hoped that collaboration would be possible.' The Archbishop gave permission for Ronald to go ahead; so he contacted Bishop Gordon Wheeler. In a letter of 21 May 1965 Ronald told Bishop Wheeler that it seemed stupid to deal with the matter of new texts in isolation and asked him how co-operation could be organized. He also asked if the Roman Catholic Church would like to provide an official observer for meetings of the JLG.

Bishop Wheeler replied enthusiastically about the possibility of joint work and accepted the invitation to send an observer to JLG. Then in June he invited Ronald to attend a meeting of the Roman Catholic Liturgical Translation Committee. Reporting to the Archbishop of Canterbury after the meeting, Ronald was most enthusiastic; 'They hope that we shall be able to work harmoniously over as wide a field as possible.' They had asked Ronald if he would attend all their meetings, though 'at the moment they have requested that we do not give any of this undue publicity'. This was carefully observed, and although drafts from Roman Catholic sources were considered by the Liturgical Commission, it was done 'in confidence'.

About this time, a certain amount of confusion occurred in Roman Catholic circles in the British Isles. The Scottish and Irish RC Churches produced their own ideas on the revised texts, and a meeting was held to bring representatives of each together. Then, to Ronald's disappointment, the Roman Catholics started to make a series of decisions on their own, holding a series of meetings in Rome under the auspices of the International Commission on the Liturgy (ICEL).

ICEL had its origins in a meeting held in October 1963, consisting in the first place of representatives of all Roman Catholic hierarchies of countries which used English, and the two English-speaking *periti* (Fr Frederick McManus and Fr Godfrey Diekmann) who were working on the Conciliar Commission on the Liturgy. Already, for over a year, the desirability of formal liturgical collaboration between English-speaking Roman Catholics worldwide had been discussed by bishops taking part in the Vatican Council. Archbishop Denis Hurley (who was to exert a great influence in the history of ICEL), a South African born of Irish parents, had set out a definite proposal for an international commission. The organization which emerged, consisted of an Episcopal Committee and a more widely representative Advisory Committee.

The Advisory Committee, having been given the responsibility of planning the entire programme and creating a plan, was then to execute the programme if approved by the Episcopal Committee. After widespread consultation, it was to submit its completed work – done under the administration of a secretariat – to the Episcopal Committee. The latter retained the ultimate responsibility for proposing liturgical texts for definitive approval to the parent episcopal conferences.[5] The Advisory Committee consisted of liturgical scholars and musicians, such as Frs McManus and Diekmann, Professor Finberg, and also Canon Harold Winstone – who, we shall learn, became a particular partner of Ronald's in ecumenical liturgical work. The Advisory Committee's first meeting was held in London in January 1965.

It was a further meeting of the Advisory Committee of this international body about which Professor Finberg wrote to tell Ronald about in October 1965. It would seem, the Professor told him, that the purely British initiative would be overtaken by these new developments. In the event, this did not happen; the hierarchies of Scotland, Ireland, England and Wales decided to adopt their own version 'to achieve unity within these Islands'. This common text, they decided, would serve until the International Committee produced its text. These texts had an ecumenical flavour – the Archbishop of Birmingham announced this at the time – in that Ronald had been attending the meetings of the Liturgical Translation Committee, and had given its members the comments which derived from the Liturgical Commission.

This early piece of ecumenical textual co-operation gave Ronald a taste of what might be possible in this field. He continued to keep in touch with the Liturgical Translation Committee and was invited to attend as an observer at the meetings of the National Liturgical Commission of England and Wales from 1965, where he received a warm welcome. He continued as an observer until 1974.

Invitation to the Roman-Catholic Consilium

In May 1966 came an invitation which would greatly accelerate the work of ecumenical liturgical co-operation. Although at first sight it seemed to be concerned only with Anglican–Roman relations, it did have a significant impact on wider ecumenical collaboration. The

Archbishop of Canterbury (Michael Ramsey) had just returned from his historic visit to Rome.

In a letter to Archbishop Fisher at Christmas 1960, Michael Ramsey, who was then the Bishop of Durham, had written, 'A widespread loosening of relations between us and the Romans has happened', and added, 'It will be a task of some years to make wide and good use of this.'[6] Six years later this same bishop, now himself Archbishop of Canterbury, made very good use of the changed situation by undertaking an official visit to the new pope, Paul VI. Geoffrey Fisher had visited Pope John XXIII in December 1960. 'The difference between the two visits was marked,' Ramsey's biographer notes. 'The Vatican treated Fisher's visit as unofficial, Ramsey's as official.'[7] Pope Paul VI's biographer also comments: 'Though there was only five years between the visits it seemed more like five hundred years to Colonel Robert Hornby, the Archbishop's press secretary on both occasions. If the formidable walls did not come tumbling down, the gates were wide open. While Fisher had been received in the Pope's private library, Ramsey was welcomed in the awesome and humbling setting of the Sistine Chapel.'[8]

One of the tangible results of this opening of the gates was that Bishop Willebrands of the Vatican Secretariat for Promoting Christian Unity approached Lambeth to ask if the Archbishop would appoint two observers from the Anglican Communion to the plenary session of the *Consilium ad exsequendam Constitutionem de Sacra Liturgia*, (to give the Consilium its full and what Bugnini called 'somewhat baroque title'). The Consilium was charged with the task of working out the practical consequences of the Constitution on the Liturgy (*Sacrosanctum Consilium*) which the Second Vatican Council had promulgated as one of its first actions. The first meeting at which observers were present was held in Rome from 6–14 October 1966. But in reality, the initiative had been taken earlier – due to Ronald's contacts.

In his *The Reform of the Liturgy 1948–1975*, Archbishop Annibale Bugnini ('the architect of the whole process of liturgical reform')[9] says: 'At the audience on December 2, 1965, Cardinal Lercaro, president of the Consilium, gave the Pope a statement in which he said that some members of the Anglican Communion who were involved in the revision of that Church's liturgy had let it be known by indirect channels that they would be interested in following the work of the Consilium at close hand.'[10] Who those members of the

Anglican Communion were Bugnini does not state, but the answer is in a letter to Ronald from Dom Hilaire Marot OSB, with whom he had been in contact for a little while. As an adviser to the Consilium, Marot had been told to produce a study of the Anglican Lectionary and had been to London to work with Ronald as had Dom Godfrey Diekmann earlier. Dom Hilaire wrote in June 1966, just before Ronald set off to his first meeting of the Consilium: 'At the last session [of the Consilium] at the end of April, on the last day I suggested in the presence of Mgr Bugnini, the Secretary of the Consilium, that the time seemed to be ripe for the invitation of observers, specially from the Anglican Communion ... and I mentioned in particular the Joint Liturgical Group of which you were the Secretary ... your name being already well known to the members of the *Coetus* that received from you the document concerning your own work.'

Ronald attended the Consilium in Rome along with Dr Massey Shepherd, Professor of Liturgy at the Church Divinity School of the Pacific, Pastor F. W. Kunneth of the Lutheran World Federation, Brother Max Thurian of Taizé, and the Revd A. Raymond George who had been appointed as an observer by the World Council of Churches. Raymond George has described that first visit:

> I well remember the first such journey in 1966. We had as a companion on the plane a veteran Roman Catholic liturgiologist, Canon R. Pilkington, who was a *peritus* at the Consilium. As the plane approached Rome he was plainly excited, partly at the sight of the city and partly at the prospect of the reform of the liturgy, which he said would soon be so changed as to be almost entirely acceptable to us all. I think he was envisaging a vernacular version in the style of Cranmer. Ronald was not to betray much emotion, but I think we all had a sense of making history.[11]

In an appreciation that Raymond George contributed to the book of essays dedicated to Ronald's memory, *Liturgy in Dialogue*, produced in 1993 by Paul Bradshaw and Bryan Spinks (two of Ronald's research students), he recalled:

> The Consilium was a large and impressive body, consisting almost entirely of cardinals and bishops, but with many *periti* in attendance, who could be called to speak but could not vote. We took no part in the

> discussions, but Archbishop Bugnini records: 'They were the first to arrive at the meetings, the last to leave the hall. They were always affable, polite, sparing of words, and ready to engage in a friendly way in any conversation that might be requested.' That certainly describes Ronald's style very well.[12]

In a report which Raymond George made to Dr Lukas Visher in Geneva, the Methodist scholar observed:

> I probably speak for all in saying that we were very much impressed by the meetings; the profound scholarship of the experts, the charity and courtesy of the debates, the willingness of so many to give so much time to the work, the ample secretarial staff all contributed to this impression. The theological differences which obviously exist between Romans and others did not loom large in these proceedings; in many, though not all, liturgical discussions they are irrelevant. Just as at Montreal the section on worship was able to proceed in considerable harmony, so here we had a strong feeling that liturgists in all the churches are faced with the same questions and are finding largely the same answers. The zeal, however, with which our Roman brothers are pursuing their work should act as a stimulus to other churches.

There was another aspect of liturgical co-operation in which the Roman Catholics were anxious to involve Ronald. This was the matter of the lectionary. The Archbishop of Canterbury had asked Ronald if he could go to a meeting in Neuberg, Austria, of one of the Consilium study groups – the *Coetus* to which Dom Hilaire's letter refers – dealing with this matter. Examinations at King's prevented Ronald attending, but he provided material about the current work of JLG on the subject through the good offices of Canon Pilkington of Westminster Cathedral. Dom Cipriano Vagaggini OSB, the 'relator' of the *Coetus*, wrote and thanked him, and told him in confidence that there was a growing realization among Roman scholars of the need to work closely with 'les autres Confessions Chretiennes'. It was, 'L'opinion privée des membres de notre Commission a été unanimé à exprimer le désir que ces contacts soient poursuivis.' This was from one of whom it had been said that 'only history will be able to detail and evaluate his efforts at every stage in the work of the preparatory and conciliar commissions responsible for the *Constitution on the Liturgy* and in the postconciliar liturgical commission.'[13] It was an important word of support for Ronald's own work in encouraging liturgical co-operation between the churches.

The matter of lectionary co-operation has limped on over the years. Way back in 1966 the Roman Catholic Consilium had hesitated over revising the readings at Mass because those lections were those which they had more or less in common with Anglicans and Lutherans. Assured by the observers that there were already plans for a new two-year lectionary drawn up by the Joint Liturgical Group, the Roman Catholics decided to go ahead, and subsequently provided their own three-year lectionary.[14] The Church of England, and in so far as they use a lectionary, the British Free Churches and the Church of Scotland, adopted the JLG lectionary in the 1960s. However, those who met at Rome during the Consilium sessions always had the hope that there would be just one lectionary. It was an ideal which must not be lost sight of, the non-Roman observers declared in 1966. More recently the work on the *Common Lectionary* has brought this ideal nearer to fruition.[15]

Ronald continued to attend meetings in Rome until 1970. In May 1969 the Congregation for Divine Worship came into being, and the Consilium became part of it as *Commissio specialis ad instaurationem liturgicae perficiendam* (a Special Commission for Completion of the Liturgical Reform). But the work was drawing to a conclusion, and in April 1970 the final meeting was held, which included a 'farewell party' in the new offices of the Congregation in Piazza Pio XII. During the proceedings there Ronald made a speech on behalf of the observers. Massey Shepherd, in a report to the Archbishop of Canterbury (17 April 1970) said that 'he spoke on behalf of all the Observers of our gratitude for this unprecedented privilege of sharing with our Roman Catholic friends in the prodigious tasks of liturgical renovation.' The next day the Commission was received by the Pope, and His Holiness Paul VI, spoke to each of the observers individually.

International consultation on English texts

We must return to the matter of 'Englishing the liturgy' as was the current, not altogether elegant, Roman Catholic phrase. While in Rome, some of the English-speaking (non-Roman Catholic) observers had been attending the meetings of ICEL. Ronald described the atmosphere on these occasions: 'Here, when texts such as those of the Lord's Prayer and the Creeds were being discussed we were treated as collaborators rather than observers, and we soon reached tentative agreement on new translations of the Gloria in Excelsis and the Apostles' and Nicene Creeds.'[16]

The Church of England Liturgical Commission had produced a series of *Modern Liturgical Texts* in time for the Lambeth Conference of 1968, and had asked for comments and criticisms both from the provinces of the Anglican Communion and from the Free Churches of this country. But in America, as a result of a Lutheran initiative led by Herbert F. Lindemann – of the Lutheran Missouri Synod Church – three church bodies, the Inter-Lutheran Commission on Worship, the Commission on Worship of the Consultation on Church Union, and the North American representatives on ICEL, had come together to form the Consultation on Common Texts (CCT). Like the JLG this was a well-informed body of officially appointed representatives, and between 1967 and 1969 they reached agreement on modern texts of the Lord's Prayer, the Apostles' and Nicene Creeds, the Gloria in Excelsis, and the Sanctus. Their work, sent to the various Liturgical Commissions on the other side of the Atlantic, had a mixed reception. For instance, the recommended version of the Lord's Prayer was not widely followed. Professor Massey Shepherd confessed (17 December 1968), 'I suspect we shall have to do much more work at the international level before we can come up with a solution that will be acceptable.'

By now there was considerable overlapping of membership of ICEL, CCT, JLG and the Consilium observers. Largely as a result of the energy of Dr Gerald A. Sigler, the secretary of ICEL, a meeting was held in London from 19–21 April 1969, at which members of all four groups met and formed themselves into the International Consultation on English Texts (ICET): yet another gathering of highly skilled and officially appointed representatives. They met for five years, until 1974, and ICEL generously provided the secretariat and made all the arrangements. Ronald said of ICET that,

> It was an untidy group, with a hard core of about twenty members. With no funds of our own, meetings had to be geared to meetings of ICEL, but it all worked effectively and the representation was wide. Members came from England, Ireland, Scotland, Wales, USA, Canada, and Australia, representing Anglicans, Roman Catholics, Lutherans,

> Baptists, Methodists, Presbyterians, Congregationalists and Church of Christ. Harold Winstone and I were elected joint chairmen, and we chaired alternate meetings. In addition we had to do a great deal of work by correspondence, collecting and reviewing a great deal of work done by smaller widely-scattered groups e.g. S. Africa and Australia, but also trying to resolve issues by quite a complicated system of postal voting – there was one particular case of four optional votes on 21 different points. It needed tact, patience and good humour and Harold [Winstone] had all three, far more than I had.[17]

The result of all their labours emerged in three editions of a booklet, *Prayers We Have in Common* – which appeared in English and American editions. Once again, as with JLG material, Ronald and his co-workers had to sell their wares to their various constituents, and it was not always easy. 'Often we had to contend with rival texts produced by individual churches: there was resentment, too, on the part of Church authorities. In the Church of England, for example, the General Synod refused to have texts imposed on it, but reserved the right to revise them, despite pleas that allowance should be made for ecumenical considerations.' But at the end of the day what emerged was a set of texts for congregational use in the Offices and Eucharist which came into use in the main English-speaking churches throughout the world. Of the texts Ronald could rightly say, 'Whatever the imperfections, you can cross oceans and continents and church barriers and pray to God in texts which are common property. That is something to be proud of and thankful for.'

Ronald believed whole-heartedly in the project. He believed, very sincerely, that he was engaged in a project which was of great significance for the drawing together of the churches. It may be that many churches and congregations must still worship separately, but if they were only dimly aware of the fact that they were using the same versions and translations as their Christian neighbours, what a gain that must be: 'Whatever future generations may say about us – we have tried – prayerfully and conscientiously – to do what we believe to have been right, to help men worship God in a worthier and more meaningful way. It has occupied some of us – including Harold and me – for something like twenty years of our lives. I for one would not have missed it for worlds.'[18] Ronald was delighted to hear in 1983 of the formation of the English Language Liturgical Consultation which took up where ICET had left off; revising the common texts and undertaking the advocacy of the *Revised Common Lectionary*. He knew then that the cause of ecumenical liturgical co-operation was alive and well and that gave him great pleasure.[19]

Societas Liturgica

The idea of an international and ecumenical 'learned society' of liturgical scholars was the brainchild of a Dutch Reformed minister, Pastor Wiebe Vos.

As we noted at the beginning of this chapter, after the second world conference on Faith and Order in Edinburgh in 1937, its continuation committee had decided to focus its future programme around three themes – the Church, Ways of Worship, and Inter-Communion. As Bishop Oliver Tomkins observed, 'Of the three great themes, worship proved the most fruitful.'[20] So it was at a meeting of the Commission on Ways of Worship held in Baarn, The Netherlands, in 1948 that Pastor Vos proposed the foundation of an Ecumenical Centre for liturgical research, the launching of an international ecumenical journal, and the formation of a society which would bring together liturgical scholars from all churches and all nations. The journal *Studia Liturgica* appeared for the first time in March 1962 under the editorship of Wiebe Vos, and he was able to create a modest Liturgical Ecumenical Centre around his pastorate in Rotterdam, the organizing of a gathering of scholars took a little longer to bring about.

In 1965 Vos and Professor J–J. von Allmen (at that time Professor of Practical Theology at the University of Neuchâtel) invited twenty-five European and American liturgical scholars to a gathering at the house of the Communauté de Grandchamp. They are a sisterhood of the Swiss Reformed Church who follow the Rule of Taizé. The theme of the conference was 'Christian Initiation', but they also took time to initiate a society. They resolved 'to found a *Societas Liturgica* i.e. an association for the promotion of ecumenical dialogue on worship, based on solid research, with the perspective of renewal and unity.'

Such aims were very near to the heart of Ronald Jasper. He was not present at the Grandchamp meeting, but was asked to be a member of a provisional council to plan the foundation meeting of the *Societas* held at the Seminary of the Reformed Church of the Netherlands at

Hydepark in Driebergen in June 1967. At that meeting, Dom Placid Murray OSB of St Columba's Abbey, Glenstal in Ireland, was elected as the first president and an Irish Anglican dean, Gilbert Mayes, became its secretary.

Dean Mayes and his wife subsequently became particular friends of the Jaspers. This was not just because Gilbert and Ronald worked together for *Societas*, but because, at about the same time, Gilbert Mayes was delegated by the Church of Ireland to be an observer at the meetings of the Church of England Liturgical Commission. It was a duty which he performed assiduously.

Dom Murray invited the new *Societas* to hold their next congress in Glenstal Abbey in September 1969. The chosen theme was 'Liturgical Language'; Ronald was asked to read one of the major papers. Before the conclusion of the congress, at the business meeting, an election was held to decide who would be the next president of *Societas Liturgica*. There was a moment of drama when it was announced that the voting had resulted in a tie! Lots were drawn and by this means Ronald was chosen as the second president of the *Societas*.

He now had to play a major part in arranging and organizing the next congress. An invitation was received from Professor Vilmos Vajta to hold the meeting in the Palais Universitaire of the Faculty of Theology of the University of Strasbourg, and members assembled there in September 1971. The chosen theme was 'Forms of Worship in the Contemporary World', and it was decided to have only two main lectures, to allow ample time for a series of workshops for planning a corporate act of worship which would conclude the congress. This decision proved to be something of a disaster. For example, many of the scholars present were far from happy to be part of a 'daisy chain' illustrating the branches of the vine. There proved to be a basic mis-match between those whose academic researches might provide crucial information about the history and fundamentals of Christian worship, and those who were willing both to consider and to demonstrate the possibilities and limitations of liturgy in contemporary worship. Those intimately involved in the affairs of *Societas* have looked back since, and realized that the infant society wobbled during the time of the Strasbourg congress. Ronald's wise guidance just about managed to keep it on an even keel, but it was a great pity that he had the bad luck to have to preside over what was not a very satisfactory conference.

The *Societas* presidency is held only for two years. After he had left that office, Ronald continued as a member of the council until 1975. He again gave a major paper at the 1977 congress held at Canterbury when the subject was 'Christian Initiation'. After this many other demands being made upon him were of a more official nature and he found that he could not spare the time to take part in further congresses of *Societas*. Consequently, it was a great joy to the more senior members that Ronald and Betty emerged from their retirement in Ripon to be the special guests of the *Societas* at the congress banquet during the meeting held at the College of Ripon and York St John, in August 1989.

NOTES

1. Horton Davies, *Worship and Theology in England*, vol. VI, *Crisis and Creativity 1965–Present*, Cambridge, 1996, p. 40ff.
2. Peter Edwall, Eric Hayman, William D. Maxwell (eds), *Ways of Worship: The Report of a Theological Commission of Faith and Order*, London, 1951.
3. Jasper, *DAL*, p. 227.
4. Adrian Hastings, *A History of English Christianity 1920–1985*, London, 1986, pp. 208–12.
5. Peter C. Finn and James M. Schellman (eds), *Shaping English Liturgy*, Washington, 1990, p. 450; J. P. Glen, *The Episcopal Contribution to the Liturgical Reform in England and Wales 1959–1984*, unpublished doctoral thesis, Institut Catholique de Paris, 1986, pp. 276–8.
6. Edward Carpenter, *Archbishop Fisher – His Life and Times*, Norwich, 1991, p. 743.
7. Owen Chadwick, *Michael Ramsey – A Life*, Oxford, 1990, p. 318.
8. Peter Hebblethwaite, *Paul VI, The First Modern Pope*, London, 1993, p. 461.
9. Hebblethwaite, *Paul VI*, p. 647.
10. Annibale Bugnini (tr. Matthew J. O'Connell), *The Reform of the Liturgy, 1948–1975*, Collegeville, 1990, p. 199.
11. Paul Bradshaw and Bryan Spinks, *Liturgy in Dialogue: Essays in Memory of Ronald Jasper*, London, 1993, p. 4.
12. Bradshaw and Spinks, *Liturgy in Dialogue*, p. 5 (cf. Bugnini, *Reform of the Liturgy*, p. 200).
13. Frederick McManus in a preface to Cipriano Vagaggini (tr. Peter Coughlan), *The Canon of the Mass and Liturgical Reform*, New York, 1967, pp. 11–12. For details of *Coetus* see Stanislaus Campbell, *From Breviary to Liturgy of the Hours, The Structural Reform of the Roman Office 1964–1971*, Collegeville, 1995, pp. 46ff.
14. Bugnini, *Reform of the Liturgy*, pp. 415–17.

15. *Common Lectionary: The Lectionary Proposed by the Consultation on Common Texts*, New York, 1983; *The Revised Common Lectionary: The Consultation on Common Texts*, Norwich, 1992.
16. These remarks by Ronald Jasper come from the typescript of a lecture. There is no indication of where (or when) it was given.
17. As note 16.
18. As note 16.
19. *Praying Together: English Language Liturgical Consultation*, Norwich, 1988, pp. 5–6.
20. *Studia Liturgica*, vol. 17, 1987, p. 8.

7

LONDON:
KING'S AND WESTMINSTER ABBEY

LIFE IN DULWICH was particularly congenial to the Jaspers while Ronald was teaching at King's. Betty enjoyed the area, the schools were good for Christine and David, and freedom from parochial or cathedral duties allowed Ronald time to prepare his university lectures, keep abreast of his work for the Joint Liturgical Group and the Liturgical Commission, and, by no means least, gave him the long-hoped-for opportunity for his own writing.

The biography of Headlam was published in 1960, and Ronald had already started work on the Life of Bishop Bell of Chichester which came out in 1967.[1] Headlam had been well received and so the book on Bell was eagerly awaited as its subject had considerably more general and popular appeal. Ronald himself was not entirely happy with the result, never feeling that he quite got under the skin of the man whom Churchill prevented from succeeding William Temple as Archbishop of Canterbury after his sudden and untimely death in 1944. Reviewers were kind, but not ecstatic. The research, as might be expected, was immaculate but there was a general feeling that more could have been extracted from the carefully documented details of the bishop's life and work. In one review, F. R. Barry, Bishop of Southwark 1941–63, thought that from time to time Ronald had allowed the historian to be slightly out of step with the biographer, and that a shorter book would have been a better biography.[2] None of which surprised Ronald, who thought that he had been rushed by Oxford University Press, and pressurized to finish the book more quickly than he would have liked, in order that it might be published before the death of Mrs Bell. This was achieved, but only by a matter of weeks. Ronald knew that this had given her great happiness and agreed it was important, but would have preferred another twelve or eighteen months to work on it.

Writing in 1967 to John Moorman, Bishop of Ripon, Ronald honestly admitted, 'I have always felt that if I were an examiner I would not have been prepared to give it more than a Beta.'

Lecturer at King's College London

Ronald could never have been described as a great common room man at King's. He did his lecturing assiduously, if not excitingly, and was loyal to the undergraduates who came to him as their academic tutor. By the system that obtained at King's for many years, each theological student was allocated a member of staff as a tutor irrespective of the lecturer's own speciality. This work he enjoyed, but academic politics generally had little interest for him, and his friendships at King's did not extend much beyond the Faculty of Theology.

Ronald's academic standards were high. Perhaps because he always valued the opportunities that higher education had given him, he had little patience with those who dissipated their energies to an extent that left inadequate time for serious study. At Leeds University he himself had enjoyed a range of sporting and musical activities, but never to the extent of losing sight of the prime objective. Not unreasonably he judged his undergraduates, not least those preparing for ordination, by his own standards. One who was an ordinand at the time (the Revd Roger Wikeley, now Rector of West Derby in Liverpool) recalls: 'He was a very demanding tutor. Whereas one could get away with things with others, not with Ronald. If you quoted a passage from a book unacknowledged you would find that he would write, not only the author and the name of the book but, frequently the page as well! He expected research for an essay to be meticulous and he was a stickler for details. At the same time, he was widely regarded as one of the nicest men on the staff of the Theological Department. He took a very real interest in his students.' Roger Wikeley admits that Ronald was not always fully appreciated by the students. 'There were those who regarded him as somewhat pedantic – e.g. he would begin his lectures almost exactly on time and he would lecture for a full fifty-five minutes. He used to love me to recall the time when he concluded his study of Confirmation by fifty minutes past the hour, and we all began to put our books away, but he was already beginning his lecture on Marriage! Indeed, Ronald frequently found amusement in my recollections of his time at King's, and one of his great assets was his ability to laugh at himself.'

There was no doubt about Ronald's academic ability, although he acknowledged his limitations. He once told Arthur Couratin somewhat disarmingly, 'I am under no delusion that I shall ever become a top grade technical liturgist in the style of Ratcliff, for I have spent too much time on other things, e.g., the Life of Headlam, Bell etc, but I do believe that I can make some contribution at this slightly lower level and in ecumenical discussion.'

Despite the demands of his work for the Commission he was able to read widely in his subject and to gather around him a number of younger scholars whose studies he guided and encouraged. One of his most distinguished students in that period, Professor Paul Bradshaw, acknowledges: 'Had it not been for Ronald, it is highly unlikely that I would ever have entered the world of serious liturgical scholarship. Not only did he facilitate my admission as a graduate student at King's College London, and supervise my doctoral research thesis, but he was also instrumental in securing the publication of my early writings and in enabling me to take my first steps in teaching the subject.'

Early in his time at King's Ronald received his doctorate of divinity from the University of Leeds. He remained loyal to his *alma mater* and sought this ultimate academic recognition from that university, rather than any other. Just before he left King's in January 1968, the University of London conferred upon him the title of Reader in Liturgical Studies. The Dean of King's, Sydney Evans, told Ronald, 'There is no doubt that your time here re-established Liturgy.' Sadly, this was not maintained and the academic study of liturgy at King's has now become as neglected there as elsewhere; a reflection on the priorities of the Church as it approaches a new century.

At the same time as his work at King's in preparing students for ordination, he was involved in the pioneering work of the Southwark Ordination Course. The course was just commencing when Ronald arrived in London. It was the first of the schemes by which men (and it was only men in those days) were able to prepare for ordination while continuing in secular employment. After ordination many remained in their jobs and were NSM's (non-stipendiary ministers) although some did go into the stipendiary ministry. One of the original 1960 students, the Revd H. C. Theobald, writes: 'I remember Dr Jasper as a very efficient lecturer, clear and straightforward. His lectures were obviously well prepared and I think we all enjoyed them – which cannot be said of some others. He was a very firm but gentle man and one felt that it was a privilege for us to sit at his feet.'

PROCTOR IN CONVOCATION

By the summer of 1964 the parliament elected in October 1959 was nearly five years old and so was fast reaching its *terminus ad quem.* When the House rose on 31 July, MPs went off thankfully to their holidays, to gird themselves for the general election in September.

In those pre-synodical days the dissolution of parliament resulted in a corresponding dissolution of the Convocations. In the subsequent ecclesiastical 'general election', Ronald was persuaded to contest the University of London seat. On 23 November Canon Sydney Evans as Returning Officer announced that Ronald had been elected by the duly qualified electors of the University of London as Proctor in Convocation in the Province of Canterbury. One of his supporters, Dr Eric Mascall, writing to congratulate him said, with typical irony, that he had just forced himself through the cheering crowds on the Embankment. 'I thought we should get you in by a judicious mixture of intimidation, bribery and doping of the electors.'

His presence in the Canterbury Convocation, and consequent membership of the Church Assembly, dovetailed nicely with his new responsibilities as chairman of the Liturgical Commission. As the volume of liturgical business increased he was available to guide it through the southern Convocation and the Assembly, and at the same time provide invaluable expertise about liturgical matters for both these legislative bodies.

'CANON JASPER'

In 1965 Ronald first became 'Canon Jasper'. He accepted the invitation of the Bishop of Derby to become 'Canon Theologian' of Derby Cathedral. This is a non-residentiary post and as the bishop said in his letter of invitation, 'it is usually held by someone competent to advise us and give us occasional help in theological matters'. He was installed in the cathedral on 11 January 1965. Ronald much enjoyed his connection with Derby Cathedral which continued until he went to York in 1975.

PUBLISHING DUTIES

Back in 1960, the Anglo-Catholic printing house, The Faith Press, advertised for a publisher. This was described as 'a part time post, requiring about 3 days of work each week'. The task was the discovering, assessing and commissioning of manuscripts for publication. In December the directors appointed Ronald to the position and he remained with Faith Press until 1965. During that time one hundred books were published, twenty-five of which were inherited from his predecessor Robin Denniston. Of the other seventy-five books, three-quarters of them were written by authors whom Ronald introduced to the Press; forty of whom were entirely new authors. Ronald reckoned that twenty-six of those books were written at his suggestion or even with his help; and that a further fifteen came through his contacts with friends or acquaintances at various universities. It meant that during his time as publisher only one book in three had been found purely and simply from among the many hundreds submitted through the post. Even so, the number of manuscripts which he needed to vet was nearly a thousand. It was described as a part-time post! By 1965 Ronald realized that he could no longer afford to allocate this amount of time to the work, and resigned. It is true that at the time there were internal personality difficulties which Ronald considered were hindering the smooth running of the Press, but he was anxious for the Board to know that although he deplored these problems, his reason for leaving was not connected with these difficulties.

CONTACTS WITH RELIGIOUS COMMUNITIES

Among those who were anxious to draw upon the advice of the lecturer in Liturgical Studies at King's London, were the religious communities of the Church of England. One of these was the Benedictine Sisters at St Mary's Abbey, West Malling. The Community had already begun to take an interest in liturgical experimentation before Ronald's first visit in August 1964, but under his influence their early experience was built upon. They admitted that before then they had known little or nothing about the liturgical movement in the Church of England as for years they had used the Benedictine Latin Office and Mass. They were *au fait* with the changes in the Roman Catholic Church and the thrust of its liturgical thinking, especially through the periodical *La Maison-Dieu* of the Centre de Pastorale Liturgique in Paris. So it was something of a novelty and extremely interesting for them to meet Ronald, and to hear what was happening in the Church of England. He went to the Abbey again in Feburary 1965, when he was able to stay the night and be present at the Community liturgy. Afterwards, he spoke to the Community about the evidence for a hymn of praise at the end of the anaphora, and suggested they should try concluding the Eucharistic Prayer with the Sanctus, telling them about E. C. Ratcliff's work on the anaphora in the *Apostolic Tradition.*[2] They adopted the suggestion and this then became a feature of the liturgy at West Malling.

Arising out of this connection, and with the encouragement of the Abbess, Dame Osyth OSB, Ronald took the Liturgical Commission to West Malling in October 1965 and for a few years it was one of the regular meeting places of the Commission. Many members of the Commission felt that some of its best work was done in the peace and serenity of the Abbey. It was in the chapel at West Malling that Series Three Holy Communion was celebrated for the very first time, with Ronald presiding and the present writer assisting. Sister Perpetua Towell OSB remembers that occasion and their other contacts with Ronald:

> In 1971 the Liturgical Commission celebrated their liturgy in our church on two successive days and invited us to be present and to make any comments and suggestions. I am sure we did, but whether any of them were accepted we never knew. The Commission continued to meet at Malling during the seventies but as their numbers increased we were no longer able to accommodate them. We gradually lost touch with Dr Jasper but we were always grateful for the years in which we knew him. I think he saw our liturgy, and the interest it aroused, as helping towards acceptance of the Church of England's new rite. Though the theory of the Sanctus as the conclusion of the anaphora of Hippolytus is no longer tenable, we are grateful to Dr Jasper for his suggestion and have retained it in the Malling rite. He had his ideas and we equally had ours so that our meetings were lively and interesting and he certainly helped us to be aware of the Church of England's liturgy and all the difficulties that a new one would involve.

'I continue to be concerned about the weight of your work at King's and in the Liturgical Commission,' wrote Archbishop Coggan to

Ronald from Bishopsthorpe, York on 14 May 1968. And then went on, 'So far, the practical outcome of my concern does not seem to have materialized – but we continue to hope it will!' In the event neither the Archbishop nor Ronald had to wait much longer. Only weeks later, the prime minister (Harold Wilson) wrote to Ronald offering to nominate him to the Queen to fill the canonry of Westminster which had become vacant due to the death of Bishop Joost de Blank.

Canon of Westminster

On the news of his acceptance the Dean of Westminster, Eric Abbott, wrote to say that he was very thankful that Ronald had decided to accept the prime minister's nomination to Her Majesty. 'I hope that your coming here will be happy for you and your family and good for the Abbey.' Ronald was not unknown to the dean. Five years earlier he had invited him to give the Gore Memorial Lecture in the Abbey and in 1966, Eric Abbott had particularly asked Ronald to speak to his personal discussion group on the subject of liturgical revision. The appointment was welcomed at Lambeth Palace. His old friend Archbishop Michael Ramsey wrote to say: 'I want to say how very glad I am that you are going to be Canon of Westminster. You will love the opportunity of sharing in the worship of a lovely house of God and of seeing the church in the ways which your office will make possible.'

The installation took place on St James's Day 25 July 1968. The installation of a canon of Westminster is a fairly low-key affair. It takes place during Evensong, although the new canon is not brought into the church until after the first lesson. He then takes a Latin oath, is installed by the dean, again in Latin, and then after the Magnificat reads the second lesson. Apart from a slight variation in the versicles and responses after the Creed, the service is little different to the normal daily service. The ceremony was followed by a reception in St Catherine's Chapel garden.

Each of the canons of Westminster has particular jobs, although strictly speaking only for a year at a time. All appointments (including archdeacon and sub-dean) are either made or renewed at the annual audit chapter. The appointment of sub-dean is made annually by the dean on that occasion, the other posts by vote of the full chapter.

On arrival Ronald became *Lector Theologiae*. At that time the principal duty was the organizing of the Lent, Advent and Trinity Lectures. The Lent Lectures were normally given by members of the chapter while the other two series were undertaken by outsiders. During his time at Westminster, Ronald served a term as Steward: the canon who is responsible for all the Abbey hospitality and, by extension, its ministry to visitors. He was also chairman of the ornaments committee, the typography committee and the music committee. He was a little disappointed not to be appointed sub-dean in 1973 when Max Warren left, but enjoyed his brief period from 1974, until his departure to York the following year, as Archdeacon of Westminster.

The demands made on his time from the wider church certainly did not decrease during his time at the Abbey, but from that base some things were more easily undertaken, not least meetings in Church House. For the first six years at Westminster the Jasper's lived in 1 Little Cloister. The first occupant of this house in 1676, after its conversion from being part of the monastic infirmary, had been Simon Patrick. Patrick (1626–1707) wrote a number of significant works on the sacraments, particularly *Mesa Mystica*, a substantial work on the Eucharist. This fact has evoked from Bishop Kenneth Stevenson the observation that

> Additional responsibilities followed in 1675 when he (Patrick) was made Canon Treasurer, he and his wife moving into 1 Little Cloister, as the first occupants of a dwelling that has housed a liturgist or two in its time.[3]

Not realizing that a new job was in the offing, the Jasper's moved in 1974 from 1 to 5 Little Cloister, in order to provide more suitable accommodation for Betty Jasper's mother, who was living with them.

From Little Cloister, Ronald still kept up his already hectic programme of speaking and preaching about liturgical developments both in the Church of England and at the ecumenical level. The only constraint was now those three months of the year when he had to be 'in residence' in the Abbey. None the less, he took every possible opportunity to explain and advocate those changes which were taking place in the worship of the Church. All invitations, from whatever source, whether seemingly insignificant or possibly important, were never declined if there was any chance they could be fitted in. Consequently, an invitation to speak in Wigan lay alongside a summons to spend a weekend at Sandringham. There he preached, and talked to the Queen and other members of the Royal Family about the task that the Church had laid upon him, with his usual clarity and coherence.

That same clarity and coherence was a feature of his sermons. Ronald was not a great preacher, but his sermons were always very carefully and prayerfully prepared, and could therefore make a deep impression. Evidence that that was so, comes from no less a witness than W. R. Matthews. As Dean of St Paul's, he had graced the pulpit of that great church from 1934 to 1967 with considerable distinction, and so would not have lightly penned this letter to Ronald:

> Just a word of gratitude for your sermon on Sunday morning, I really rejoiced over it. I was back in the days when the pulpit of the Abbey was a power in the land – and other pulpits too. In my student days Hensley Henson and R. J. Campbell were drawing multitudes to hear thought-provoking discourses and I learned a lot. I do hope that you will continue in this great and needed ministry to the 'intellectuals' hovering between 'yes' and 'no'. Alas not a few sermons today which are intended to say 'yes' actually favour 'no' by the poverty of their thought. By the way, Hensley Henson once told me that he never spent less than 5 hours in preparing a sermon. All good wishes – don't cut down the sermon – the Abbey has a special opportunity.

Just before he left the deanery of Westminster, Eric Abbott left on record his opinion that Ronald Jasper ought to have 'a job of his own'. The dean said, 'He has a definite mind of his own and I do not think he should stay at Westminster much longer.' The dean particularly suggested a See in the north of England. However, it was not a diocesan bishopric in the province of York that Downing Street had in mind for Ronald, but the deanery of its Metropolitical Cathedral.

NOTES

1. Ronald C. D. Jasper, *George Bell, Bishop of Chichester*, London, 1967.

2. A. H. Couratin and D. H. Tripp (eds), E. C. Ratcliffe, *Liturgical Studies*, London, 1967, pp. 18–37.
3. Kenneth Stevenson, *Covenant of Grace Renewed: A Vision of the Eucharist in the Seventeenth Century*, London, 1994, p. 150.

8

THE ALTERNATIVE SERVICE BOOK

RONALD JASPER PROBABLY would not have expected that his biography would ever be written. His modesty, I suspect, would have led him to compare the scale of his life's achievements with those whose careers he had chronicled in the works of biography that he so much enjoyed writing. However, that would be the assessment of the modest man that he was. His achievements were far from insignificant and culminated in the publication of The Alternative Service Book in 1980.

He knew, indeed he had studied and written, about the frustrations of those involved in previous attempts at liturgical revision. Equally, he was seized by the urgency and importance of producing an authorized and completely legal alternative to The Book of Common Prayer. Even in the comparatively few years since the publication of ASB there are far too many who have forgotten, and sadly many who do not know, that for years the parish churches of England were trapped in a liturgical situation which was completely unacceptable. Some thought they could find their way out of the dilemma by adopting the formularies of other churches, principally (if not exclusively) those of the Roman Catholic Church. Others tinkered to a greater or lesser extent with The Book of Common Prayer and tried to do their best with it. It was widely appreciated that the situation was unsatisfactory, but there seemed little that could be done about it. There was the somewhat pathetic attempt of the *Shorter Prayer Book*, and the less well known *People's Prayer Book*, but they solved very little. Meanwhile, the wedding, baptism and funeral services from the parliamentary-rejected 1928 book were widely and almost exclusively used, despite their tenuous legal status.

The Parish Communion movement which swept through the Church of England in the 1950s and 1960s found parishes attempting to use an order for Holy Communion which could hardly bear the burden they were placing upon it. This movement, which attracted support across a broad band of churchmanship, highlighted the inadequacies of contemporary Church of England liturgy.

What a breath of liturgical fresh air began to blow through the Church of England from the mid-1960s, when the first fruits of the work of the Liturgical Commission became available! At the first Liturgical Conference, organized in 1966 by the Church Assembly in order to give a platform for the Commission's proposals, Archbishop Ramsey introduced the Series One services. These, in the main, were versions of those 1928 services which had been so long (unofficially) in use, although the service of Holy Communion was 1928 considerably modified and improved, even at the expense of a large number of alternatives. Those present in Church House on 18 February 1966, who were aware of the long history of eucharistic controversy in the Church of England, were anxious to hear propositions on tackling further revision of the Holy Communion service. They had in front of them what the Commission described as 'a draft Order', rather than a polished and finished service. On behalf of the Commission, Canon Arthur Couratin told the conference: 'It might be best if I began by telling you how we started producing the draft. We were, all of us, thinking in terms of a parish communion, that is to say a Sunday Service, with a sermon, and the bulk of the congregation communicating.'[1] Couratin was describing the beginning of a long process, many of the details of which we have already traced in Ronald's life; but there is no doubt that the crowning achievement for him would be the publication of a fully authorized book produced on this basis, with these practical and pastoral principles.

Birth of the ASB

By 1971, Ronald was convinced the pace of revision was such that he could propose that the energies both of the Commission and the Synod might now be focused on the production of 'an Alternative Prayer Book'. In a letter to the Archbishop of Canterbury in March of that year he included this proposal in an eight-point plan. In this schedule, 1662 would remain unchanged and continue to be available, whereas the Series One and Two services (with the possible exception of Series One Holy Communion) should be allowed to lapse. The new book should be produced in two forms, Ronald believed; a full edition and a shorter version containing only the material for Morning and Evening Prayer and Holy Communion.

At that time he believed the work could be completed by 1975–76 and that it could be achieved without recourse to parliament, as long as the new Worship and Doctrine Measure was passed. This particular piece of ecclesiastical legislation was aimed at giving the Church of England control over the content of its services. Ronald was anxious that, at the same time, the Church should retain control over the printing and publishing of those services.

The printing, design and typographical presentation of liturgical texts remained another preoccupation of Ronald's. Back in 1968, with the help and encouragement of John Wilkinson, he had organized a top-level meeting of all interested parties with the Archbishop of Canterbury, to discuss the whole matter of the visual presentation of services. Perhaps the important outcome of this meeting was the decision to engage Keith Murgatroyd, at that time president of the Society of Typographic Designers, as independent designer. Murgatroyd's first project was the 'Report of Holy Communion Series Three', and he worked with Ronald and others on the printing and publishing of all subsequent services through to the production of the ASB. In this matter Archbishop Ramsey gave his personal support, writing to Ronald in February 1972 to say, 'It is certainly our hope that Mr Murgatroyd's design will continue to be used, for it gives the printed service a quality of helpfulness to worshippers in church which is greatly appreciated.' Ronald himself was of the opinion that the attention given to good typography served to underline the fact that the printed word itself can be recognized as having its own unique contribution to liturgical revision. Robin Brookes, who was SPCK's editorial manager at that time, and not keen on the idea of using Murgatroyd, recalls ruefully: 'In (I think) April 1972 the publishers were called to a meeting of the Archbishops' Advisers on Liturgical Copyright. Over lunch at 1 The Sanctuary we met with David Carey the Provincial Registrar, Sir John Guillum Scott the Secretary-General of the Synod, and Bishop Geoffrey Tiarks, the Archbishop's Senior Chaplain. Derek Pattinson, then Sir John's associate and designated successor, was also present. Ronald Jasper was there to make the case for staying with Murgatroyd, and it was clear that he had already obtained the backing in advance of both Archbishops.'

The Synodical processes

Derek Pattinson succeeded Sir John Guillum Scott as Secretary General of the Synod in November 1972. He had worshipped at the Grosvenor Chapel for many years, while serving as a senior civil servant in HM Treasury, and had developed a keen interest in the production of good liturgy. Over the next eight years he afforded Ronald valued support and encouragement both administratively and personally. Derek Pattinson produced an important report in 1973 entitled *The Future Course of Liturgical Revision.* In it, among other proposals, he suggested the setting up of a working party to plan what was now called a 'People's Service Book'.[2] In the subsequent Synod debate in July of that year, the proposal for a working party was accepted with considerable enthusiasm, whereas an amendment to change the title to 'Book of Common Prayer 1980' was rejected. However, the target date of 1980 was criticized by both Archbishops. Archbishop Ramsey was particularly severe in his remarks, saying that the pastoral need was urgent and he hoped that the book would be in the hands of people 'really soon – I would hope within two years from now, not more that'.

Although he himself had suggested a completion date of 1975–6, Ronald was well aware of the huge amount of work that still needed to be done. He decided not to intervene on this point, in the Synod debate, not wanting either to start an argument which he felt was unnecessary, or to dampen the Synod's obvious enthusiasm for a new book. In the event it was six months before the working party was set up and any hope of an earlier completion date quickly disappeared. The working party was a small body of twelve, with Ronald and David Silk representing the Commission and John Habgood, at that time Bishop of Durham, as chairman. Of the experience of working with Ronald at this time Lord Habgood has written: 'As Chairman of the Committee I was acutely conscious of the key role which Ronald played in it and the firmness of his own ideas about what sort of book it should be. It is important to make the point, however, that the actual contents of the book which determined its size and complexity were decided after a questionnaire had been sent to a representative sample of parishes. In other words we gave the parishes what they asked for and were not being doctrinaire about what we ourselves thought the ASB ought to contain.' The former archbishop goes on to clarify another point on which there has been persistent misunderstanding concerning the relationship between the ASB and the BCP. He says: 'Our initial discussions with the privileged presses, largely at Ronald's instigation, made it clear that the incorporation of any BCP material into the ASB would throw serious doubt on the ability of the privileged presses to go on producing the full BCP. It was thus in the interests of keeping our promises that the BCP would continue to be published that we were driven to exclude BCP material from the ASB, with the result that the Committee and Ronald, in particular, were accused of trying to supress BCP material.'

Lord Habgood believes it was important to mention these points to illustrate the kind of issues which the committee had to face, and the great influence which Ronald had in policy decisions, as well as in the enormously intricate and detailed work of editing the text in order to turn a multitude of different services into a coherent book. It was not an easy time. Dr Habgood recalls, 'Both of us suffered a good deal of flak when interim reports were debated by the Synod, and I look back on it as a time of very fruitful co-operation with a colleague who had enormous expertise and yet was willing to work very graciously with amateurs in the field like myself!'

The relationship was one of mutual respect; Ronald commenting that although John Habgood described himself as 'a reluctant liturgical reviser' he was a first-class chairman. Ronald was certain that the archbishop possessed the qualities necessary for that particular difficult and delicate venture: toughness, fairness, patience, and a grasp of detail.[3] By the time the working party reported to the Synod in 1975 it had the benefit of the replies received by means of a questionnaire which had been sent out to 620 parishes. Once again Ronald's keenness to canvas 'the grass roots' came to the fore.

On the basis of the information they obtained from the questionnaire, the working party now firmly proposed that the result of these long years of liturgical revision should culminate in the publication of an 'Alternative Service Book' – and the title 'People's Service Book' was dropped. Such a book would not contain any 1662 material (for the reasons that Lord Habgood has explained), but would include a full range of alternative services together with a liturgical psalter.

The working party's report contained the fascinating information that the pew editions of Series Two Holy Communion had sold nearly three million copies, and that by June 1975, the Series Three service had sold well over a million and was selling at twice the rate of Series Two. What better evidence could there be of the hunger of parishes for something more suitable to their needs?

In a subsequent debate in February 1976, the General Synod agreed to accept the proposal that the Bishop of Durham made to them, on behalf of the working party, that a much smaller group, still under his chairmanship, should be set up to supervise the final stage of the book. To this group Ronald acted as the link between the Church and the publishers and as what he described as 'general editorial dogsbody'.

The year 1979, in which Ronald was much involved in the final work on the new service book, was also the last year in office of Donald Coggan as Archbishop of Canterbury (Ronald's predecessor as chairman of the Commission). Ronald had always worked easily with Dr Coggan and they had a mutual respect for each other's gifts. Ronald looked back with his historian's eye on the comparatively brief four years that Donald Coggan had occupied the Commission's chair, as the time when the Commission had recovered its sense of purpose and direction and significantly broadened its horizons. He knew that he would miss the certainty of Archbishop Coggan's strong, steadying influence and his readily available sympathetic ear. Ronald wrote later, 'I can only say that I missed him greatly.' Lord Coggan has subsequently stated his own immense admiration for Ronald's complete and singleminded commitment to this task, vital to the future of the Church of England. He has said, 'I admired his tenacity and the way he handled the Synod.'

Detailed work on the ASB

This commitment was to be severely tested in those final years of work on the ASB. The 'general editorial dogsbody' needed to undertake many tasks. Primarily, there was his continuing work as chairman of the Liturgical Commission. That was by no means confined to moderating full meetings many days each year, but also involved hours of letter writing regarding particular problems. For instance, two of these occupied a good deal of time and energy – although either might qualify as one of those fictional subjects of which it is said, 'They talk of little else in Heckmondwike.' One was the continuing debate on the anamnesis–oblation in the Eucharistic Prayer; and the other the efforts to solve the problem of the ninth line in the Lord's Prayer. Support for the proposed ICET (and therefore international and ecumenical) proposal for the latter, 'save us from the time of trial' was, to say the least of it, lukewarm.

Add to these responsibilities not only the meetings of the Synod; the work of the publishing group; regular meetings with the House of Bishops and his own continuing drafting of material – but also his secretaryship of the Joint Liturgical Group, and other ecumenical projects, and you gain something of a picture of Ronald's workload. And then there was York Minster.

No wonder some Minster folk suggested their dean was more likely to be discovered on the platform of York station than anywhere else. This was not only untrue, but unkind. Never during this hectic time did Ronald neglect his decanal duties, but how he managed to keep all the various balls in the air during that period can only be a matter for amazement and admiration.

As the amount of liturgical business which had to go through the synodical process increased, new procedures were introduced. Each service had its own 'steering committee' on which the Liturgical Commission was always represented, and this committee was included in a revision committee which considered all the amendments that were submitted. At first these amendments were few, and the committee could complete its work in a couple of sessions. Later, as Ronald put it, 'the submission of amendments became almost a synodical obsession; they could number hundreds for a single service and on one occasion, exceeded a thousand.'[4] It was proving a very expensive operation and many, like Ronald, doubted whether it was an ideal method of creating good liturgy. Colin Buchanan thought it was a system unique upon earth, and worthy of a place in the *Guinness Book of Records* for the amount of hours spent, the number of amendments proposed and the amount of verbiage produced on each of the services. Of this particular process the Bishop of Winchester, John Taylor, speaking in the Synod, said, 'I have thought increasingly through the whole process that this is something which I hope our Church will never do again. This is not the way to write liturgy.'[5]

At first Ronald was inevitably appointed as the chairman of each steering committee, but as the number of these increased and overlapped one with another, the constraints on his time impelled a change. So, as the detailed work on the production of the Alternative Service Book multiplied, he wisely decided to leave the business of the steering and revision committees to other members, or even former members, of the Commission. For example, and not surprisingly, the revision committee for Holy Communion Series Three was flooded with amendments, not only from members of the Synod but from many groups and organizations outside. This needed expert guidance because so much else in the ASB would pivot upon decisions made over this service. Fortunately Bishop Cyril Bowles, former vice-chairman of the Commission, was willing to undertake the task to Ronald's great relief and pleasure. They shared a mutual respect and Bishop Bowles has commented:

> Ronald had a clear vision of the direction in which the Church of England should go, but he was not assertive over his ideas nor about the details that the revision of its services should take. Along with his fine powers of mind he had wide sympathies and made an excellent chairman. He listened to others and helped all the members to be listeners themselves. He was never partisan and was an inspiration to his colleagues, whether as individuals or working in small groups. He worked exceedingly hard and never lacked the necessary knowledge on any question.

Some of this knowledge Ronald harnessed into publications which explained in a simple and straightforward way what the Commission was attempting to achieve. In writing these he was joined by other members who added their expertise. Principally, there was *The Eucharist Today*, a set of studies on Series Three which was published in 1974, and a *Commentary* on the ASB, which appeared in 1980.

Throughout this period of intense activity, with constant journeyings up and down the country, the daily need to be tackling yet another query, the sheer enormity of the task and the responsibility for it, Ronald remained remarkably unflappable. His main source of irritation was when others failed to give to these matters the commitment which he thought they deserved, or failed to keep to deadlines. His immediate colleagues, to whom he paid the highest tribute, were equally wholehearted. He led a remarkably dedicated team.

Ronald admitted that at times the pressures were considerable, but even then he did not lose his commendable knack of knowing how and when to 'switch off'.

Those who had only seen the somewhat schoolmasterly Dr Jasper at the podium in Church House, or perhaps as a visiting lecturer giving a highly knowledgeable but not necessarily exciting address on liturgical revision, would perhaps have failed to recognize him in the convivial company of a small group of his fellow-commissioners in the bar of the village inn in Appletreewick. He could be found enjoying a pint of Old Peculiar at the end of a hard day spent revising, changing, testing, and then perhaps amending again some part of the future liturgy of the Church of England. And not just in the lovely Yorkshire Dales: it might equally have been in a quiet pub just outside West Malling Abbey or not far from St Stephen's House Oxford, or down the road from St Peter's Woking, or in any one of those places to which the Commission went to do its important work.

The conversation on those occasions was not usually liturgical, they had had enough of that; but it was often ecclesiastical. As with any group of clergy there was always a good deal of discussion about who was going where, who indeed ought to go there, and who stood no chance of going anywhere. It was immensely good-humoured, based on very little special knowledge, yet relaxing and unwinding.

At home, Ronald had his own method of relaxation which he was not in the least bit ashamed to admit – he enjoyed watching television and listed it among his recreations in *Who's Who*. He did not try to justify himself by saying it kept him in touch with the wider world of contemporary communication: he watched because he was entertained and relaxed by it. Indeed he would rarely work long, if at all, after his evening meal. Having applied himself wholeheartedly during the day, he was now content to watch TV. Sometimes house guests were taken aback by the almost contradictory strictness of this rule of leisure, but Ronald obviously reaped its benefits, not least in the last hectic years before the publication of the ASB.

THE NEW RITE IS LAUNCHED

The General Synod of the Church of England is elected for five-year periods. It is not inevitably tied to parliamentary elections as in the days of the Church Assembly. During the summer of 1980 there was a synodical 'general election' and the newly elected body was summoned to Westminster on 12 November. Two days before, The Alternative Service Book was published and was used for the Synod's opening service in Westminster Abbey in the presence of Her Majesty the Queen. The Bishop of Manchester (Patrick Rodger) was moved to suggest that during the service the assembled congregation should have sung (to the tune 'Westminster Abbey'),

> All its walls are made of Jasper,
> Clear as crystal, free from stain,
> Naught that's cumbrous, naught archaic,
> Here is suffered to remain,
> Lest the Lord misunderstand us,
> Let's address him plain as plain.

After the service the Queen inaugurated the new Synod in Church House, following which the Archbishop of York (Stuart Blanch) presented her with a copy of the ASB. Dr Blanch commented as he did so:

> The Alternative Service Book is not, as ill-informed comment might suggest, a substitute for, but an alternative to, The Book of Common Prayer. In order to make this particular point it was suggested at one stage that I might present to you at the same time a copy of The Book of Common Prayer in a matching binding. But, Your Majesty, I presume that you already have a copy, and – not to make too fine a point of it – as a multiple parishioner of the Church of England you might demur at what might seem to be a needless extravagance.[6]

Ronald was quietly proud of the fact that his work was recognized six months later in the New Year's honours list, when he was appointed Commander of the Most Excellent Order of the British Empire. He was less pleased with the recognition given to others who had laboured long and hard alongside him. In particular, he thought that the Lambeth BD – rather than a doctorate – awarded to Charles Whitaker was bordering on the insulting. Charles had spent an enormous amount of time on the massive operation of ordering the calendar and putting the Office and Eucharistic lectionaries into one coherent system. Charles also produced courses of psalmody, rules to order the service, tables of movable feasts, and the date of Easter for the next fifty years. All this from one who had been brought on to the

Commission because of his immense erudition in initiation matters. It was no wonder that the Commission knew the resulting report as 'Whitaker's Almanac'. Ronald thought that the offer of a BD was less than gracious, but was not surprised that phlegmatic Charles accepted it with no more than an old-fashioned look as he puffed away at his pipe.

Ronald was always acutely aware of the need to use the talents of others. For example, his willingness to use Murgatroyd's expertise; his setting up of a group with theatre and drama connections to look at presentational matters; the encouragement of experiments with liturgical dress and his care over musical matters by drawing on the musical expertise of Alan Wicks, John Rutter, Cyril Taylor and Lionel Dakers.

Opposition

During the last five years of work on the ASB a new element arose, with the formation of the Prayer Book Society in 1975. As a student of the history of the Book of Common Prayer, Ronald knew that this new-found 'Prayer Book fundamentalism' was a fresh phenomenon in the Church of England. Although later the Prayer Book Society modified its advertisements and propaganda to make clear that they did not exist merely to oppose the Alternative Services, but to advocate and preserve services according to the Book of Common Prayer, the overall effect was to motivate those who thought it was incumbent upon them to oppose what they chose to portray as an attack on English cultural life, and particularly its language. Around this banner gathered many who had little or no attachment to the Church of England, and perhaps not even to Christianity, but who declared themselves as being keen to defend Prayer Book language. Some thought they detected an unhelpful cultural élitism in much of this criticism. The culmination of all this backlash activity came in November 1979 when the Petition of the Six Hundred was presented to the General Synod. It appeared in the journal *PN Review 13*, surrounded by articles attacking modern versions of the Bible and modern liturgies. The petition pleaded for the 'continued and loving use in churches as part of the mainstream worship' of the Authorized Version of the Bible, and The Book of Common Prayer. Of this, Ronald commented that it was cleverly phrased and 'could have been signed with a good conscience by people who were also happy to accept a revision of the liturgy; indeed, many of the signatories had helped the Liturgical Commission over the years. But placed within the context of the journal a rather different impression was created, with reformers and those who supported them being shown in a bad light.'[7]

Ronald always realized that the matter of language was an emotive one, and although sensitive to the issues, more than once declared that he was 'not another Cranmer'. But in the same way as Cranmer unhesitatingly drew on his contemporaries to help and assist – so too Ronald was more than willing to seek advice and use it. However, he would never accept the argument that what he was doing was destructive.

The design of a new, but always alternative, Prayer Book was what he knew the overwhelming majority of regular worshipping members of the Church of England needed and were anxiously awaiting. Years of liturgical 'do-it-yourself', or even downright anarchy, had to come to an end. The soul's health of a church necessitated that it had a liturgy which was both acceptable and legal. Modern, lively congregations up and down England needed a vehicle for worship with which they could identify and so feel that their services expressed their needs and aspirations. The Prayer Book Society members, Ronald believed, looked back on an idealized past in which they imagined Anglican congregations gladly and willingly making their way through the Prayer Book services.

Yet this historian of the Prayer Book knew that not only had the years from 1662 onwards been regularly punctuated by suggestions for amendments and changes, but that there was now scarcely a parish which did not make greater or lesser changes to the official legal text of 1662. As we have already seen, there were probably only a handful of parishes which did not use the parliamentarily-rejected 1928 rites for baptism, marriage and funeral services. No parish priests would anticipate the slightest objection to the use of what were, in the strict letter of the law, illegal services. No one thought they had not been baptized, married, or their loved ones given a seemly funeral as a result of the use of these services. But it was hardly a satisfactory or honest situation for a church to live in, and now that the process of revision of canon law had been completed, there could be a better way. Yet could this 'better way' be couched in dignified and suitable English?

A modern liturgical language

To achieve an acceptable liturgical language, Ronald insisted that the Commission draw on a wide range of opinions. The first person recruited to the Commission as an acknowledged expert on language was Dr Stella Brook of Manchester University, who had just published a study on *The Language of the Book of Common Prayer*.[7] She was appointed in 1965, but only served for three years being compelled to resign owing to ill-health. Dr Brook was replaced by two people: Cyril Taylor, who was appointed in the first place as a musician but who, Ronald said, possessed 'a fine ear for sound and rhythm, with a knack of finding just the right word or phrase'; and Dr David Frost, a fellow of St John's Cambridge.

Dr Frost proved to have a real flair for liturgical writing and a particular gift for rendering the Hebrew of the Psalms into English. Later, during the last stages of the work on the ASB, David left to take up a chair in Australia and was replaced by the Professor of English Studies at the University of Nottingham, James Kinsley. Another careful user of the English language was Elisabeth Montefiore whose opinions were much respected. In this context we must not forget the many contributions of Geoffrey Cuming to the fine tuning of a phrase. All these members of the Commission sat around the table during the long hours of debate and drafting, and had constant opportunity to refine the language. Ronald also initiated an experiment of involving the Poet Laureate (C. Day Lewis) by asking him to write modern metrical versions of the canticles. They were included in a Commission publication entitled *Modern Liturgical Texts* produced in 1968. It did not produce anything of lasting value, but it did demonstrate a willingness to listen to the advice of contemporary literary practitioners of some eminence.[8]

In the years since its publication, the ASB has proved an easy target for those who like to parrot phrases about 'committee English' and 'the language of bureaucracy', but this is to forget the constraints under which Ronald Jasper and his Commission worked. For instance, the post-communion prayer, 'Father of all we give you thanks and praise', was the sole survivor, in the main text, when a number of more colourful suggestions made for inclusion in the Holy Communion failed to survive the synodical process. The lack of flowery phrases in the liturgy was what Ronald interpreted the Church in the 1970s as asking of the Commission. He was not a minimalist by choice, yet he heard contemporary stylists like Richard Hughes (author of *Fox in the Attic* and other acclaimed novels) saying such things as:

> Now make no mistake: I am not suggesting that a reformed liturgy should use the vocabulary of the *Daily Mirror* any more than it should utter the thoughts of the *Daily Mirror*. Nor am I making Ruskinian proposals that we should try to weed words of latin origin out of our vocabulary – calling an 'omnibus' a 'folkwain' and such like nonsense. What I do assert is that the modern Englishman normally thinks in short sentences almost bereft of subordinate clauses and parentheses. Again he leaves the relation between these sentences to be implied by the mere juxtaposition without any of the explanatory conjunctions so beloved of the latinist (he leaves a spark-gap for the meaning to leap rather than a connecting wire to conduct it). He certainly does not think in these immense periods punctuated by rare full-stops: why it would be truer to say that he thinks in a series of full-stops punctuated by rare words.[9]

One of the further constraints on extravagance of language lurked in the necessity to pacify those of differing churchmanship who wanted to be sure that they understood the theological implications of what the liturgy contained. This contributed to a certain straightforwardness of language. The use of too many adjectives and adverbs could serve to obscure, or even modify, the essential basic thrust of some liturgical statements within the liturgy. The much-to-be-desired spirit of 'live and let live' was unfortunately not generally accepted by die-hards of the two main ecclesio-political persuasions, and they scrutinized every word of a liturgical text to examine it for signs of doctrinal deviation. In that atmosphere beauty of language is often a discarded victim.

Yet despite all this, Ronald Jasper led his team in producing the best book that such a pondorous system was ever likely to achieve. It was not perfect; at various points it was not the book that Ronald Jasper would have chosen to set before the Church if he had had *carte blanche* – but he had not. Nevertheless, he was very much of the opinion that in the last resort, without the constant drafting and redrafting it would have been considerably less acceptable all round.

His confidence was justified and it has proved to be a splendid vehicle for the renewal and revivification of the worship of the Church of England, when used with intelligence and under-standing.

To aid such intelligent use of the book, Ronald worked with Paul Bradshaw to produce *A Companion to the Alternative Book* which gave full details of the source and intention of the material contained in the ASB.[10] This *Companion* has sold well, but the evidence of one's eyes and ears suggest that in some parishes it ought to be better known. Ronald always knew that liturgical education ('formation' was not yet the fashionable word) would always be necessary for clergy and laity if standards of worship were to be raised. Additionally, he edited a series of very practical essays by members of the Joint Liturgical Group entitled *Getting the Liturgy Right*,[11] and was greatly concerned when he observed how the subject was given lower and lower priority in theological colleges and courses.

Throughout his long labours on liturgical revision, Ronald had suffered a good deal of abuse and criticism. Despite his seeming unflappability he did not always find it easy. Canon Raymond Hockley, a colleague at York at the time of the publication of the ASB in 1980 witnessed the effect on his dean. It was not that Ronald did not expect and value criticism, says Canon Hockley. What really distressed him were the nasty, peevish letters he received, accusing him of murdering the English language and destroying faith. Often these letters were from his fellow clergy: they were not constructive, kind, charitable statements, but were deliberately cruel, calculated and intended to hurt. This Ronald could not understand. Honest and straight-forward he certainly was; perhaps occasionally lacking in sensitivity: but he was never malicious or unkind, and so found it difficult to understand it in others, particularly in church people. In such circumstances it is important to retain a sense of humour. Ronald was amused, as were the other members of the Commission, to receive a piece of gentle self-mockery circulated by one of their number in the form of an 'Anti-Memo'.

> It is therefore with some confidence that we recommend this new form of confession to Synod, with full episcopal approval : if it has not met with much enthusiasm, it can fairly be said to offend no one. We regret the lack of scriptural reference; but prayers for today cannot be written in language and imagery so dependent on the thought-patterns of the past.

Dear God,
we have been naughty,
we have been nasty,
and we are most upset;
but Jesus is our pal,
so give us a helping hand,
and we in return will promise
never to do it again. Amen.

President: The Lord says: 'don't worry, it'll be all right.'
All say: Thank God!

In a lecture he gave soon after the publication of the ASB Ronald emphasized his belief that the liturgy belongs to the whole people of God, and that it is not just a clerical preserve; also that the liturgy had to be capable of containing a number of tensions. It has to contain within itself much that is old and traditional, while seeming to be forever new and contemporary; equally it has to hold together the temporal and the eternal, the earthly and the heavenly; and finally, and frighteningly, it has to make an attempt to express in words that which is, in essence, inexpressible. For how long would the ASB be the way to attempt such a venture of faith, Ronald asked himself? Not for ever, of that he was sure, because 'one of the great discoveries is that liturgy is not a static thing, and Cranmer himself recognised this'.

Ronald Jasper knew that the ASB was only officially authorized for use until the year 2000, and would have approved of the present-day efforts which are producing new and exciting liturgical material. But he would not unreasonably have asked that it be not forgotten, amid the flurry of current activity, that he and his fellow pioneers not only 'broke the mould', but bore the burden and heat of the day over twenty-five years. He and they deserve that of the Church.

NOTES

1. *The Liturgical Conference 1966, Report of Proceedings*, 1966, pp. 70–71.
2. *The Future Course of Liturgical Revision*, Report by the Standing Committee, GS 161, 1973, p. 13.

3. Jasper, *DAL*, p. 344.
4. Jasper, *DAL*, p. 318.
5. *General Synod Report of Proceedings*, vol. 10, 1979, pp. 909–10.
6. *General Synod Report of Proceedings*, vol. 11, 1980, p. 790.
7. Stella Brook, *The Language of the Book of Common Prayer*, London, 1965.
8. Liturgical Commission, *Modern Liturgical Texts*, 1968, pp. 16–29.
9. Richard Hughes, *Liturgical Language Today*, Church in Wales Publications, Cardiff, n.d., reprinted from *Province*, vol. XIII, no. 4.
10. R. C. D. Jasper and Paul F. Bradshaw, *A Companion to the Alternative Service Book*, London, 1968.
11. R. C. D. Jasper (ed.), *Getting the Liturgy Right*, Essays by the Joint Liturgical Group, London, 1982.

9

DEAN OF YORK

APPOINTMENTS TO SENIOR posts in the Church of England are never made hastily or incautiously. Even the choice of names of candidates for preliminary consideration are the subject of the most careful scrutiny – but all in the strictest secrecy. In recent years the appointment of diocesan bishops has acquired a system deriving from James Callaghan's 'concordat'.[1] Even so, those who are under consideration for appointment have no idea that their future is being discussed, and any form of personally conducted candidacy has generally been considered as a guarantee of instant disqualification. For these most senior positions, there are still no advertised lines of communication available to those who might wish to propose a name for consideration. Under the new 'Callaghan' arrangement, the Church is officially involved in episcopal appointments; however, the choice of deans (and certain residentiary canons) is still jealously guarded by the Crown – although the advice of the Archbishops is heeded. Despite that, in the end, the choice of priest to be invited is the unfettered choice of the Sovereign, for whom the Prime Minister is the particular (and by title and definition) the *prime* adviser.

Alan Richardson died on 23 February 1975, having been Dean of York since 1964. The search for a successor began in March, and very quickly Ronald Jasper's name was being considered. On 17 March W. H. Saumerez Smith, the Archbishop's Appointments' Secretary, wrote to Colin Peterson, the Appointments' Secretary at Downing Street, saying of Ronald: 'I would regard him as a very strong candidate: scholarly, not too old, plenty of experience of the north, to which he would like to return, capitular experience too, a leading figure in the Church of England, ready for a move.'[2] Donald Coggan wrote to the Archbishop of York, supporting Saumerez Smith's suggestion and saying: 'I have seen a good deal of Ronald down the years. He succeeded me as Chairman of the Liturgical Commission and has done a quite magnificent job in that capacity.

I have always found him a genial and delightful person, and I think he has certain gifts which might mean that we ought to consider his name very seriously among others.'[3] In his response Archbishop Blanch says that, although he didn't know Ronald very well, he believed that 'he would obviously bring great gifts for our enrichment here'. In all this they were supported by Edward Carpenter, who had succeded Eric Abbot as Dean of Westminster. He had already anticipated the suggestion and writing to Archbishop Coggan Dr Carpenter said:

> It has occurred to me that perhaps Ronald Jasper might be considered for the Deanery at York. In saying that I want to make it perfectly clear that members of the Chapter, and I personally, would feel his loss tremendously from the Abbey, but I am in this context thinking of him and his own future. Ronald has energy, is deeply conscientious, and as you know has had university experience, has written books, and has been in a parish. He is certainly talented. I am sure he is worthy of consideration. Perhaps I might add that he has a very open and frank personality, and his wife is a most warm-hearted and practical person.[4]

By May, Archbishop Blanch was clear about the recommendation that he wanted to place before the Prime Minister (Harold Wilson). Of the two most likely candidates he would, on balance, favour Ronald Jasper, he says. He justified his preference to the Prime Minister thus:

> Ronald Jasper is well-known in the Church, not simply for his liturgical knowledge but for the astonishing patience he has shown over many years in piloting controversial proposals through the General Synod. He would certainly command the respect of the Chapter and his recognised position in the Church of England would be a distinct help in looking afresh at the pattern of services at present followed in York Minster. In addition he would have the advantage of having been brought up, educated and having served in the ministry in this part of the world. In particular the fact that he had been parish priest would, I believe, help to strengthen the links between the Minster and the parishes of the diocese. He is the right age and an extremely agreeable person who could be expected to get on well with the Civic Authorities and with others in positions of leadership in the County. His experience

of Westminster as amongst other things a great tourist centre would be a help in dealing with that aspect of our life here.[5]

In reply, Colin Peterson tells Stuart Blanch that the Archbishop of Canterbury has spoken to him about the appointment and has asked Peterson to let the Prime Minister know that he feels Ronald Jasper has a very strong claim.

With all this advice it is no surprise at all that the Prime Minister wrote asking Ronald if he might place his name before the Queen.

The offer came as a great delight to Ronald and Betty, not least because, as he told the Archbishop of York, 'my wife and I are absolutely devoted to the North'. But there were also problems to be solved, the first of which concerned the work of the Commission. 'I have simply given my life to this for over twenty years and now in the final run up – the last five years – the prospect of giving it all up is unthinkable. The problem is – can I run the two, even for a limited period? And I ask the question purely on physical grounds, because I am no longer indestructable (as I thought I was until two years ago!)'

Much would turn on the York set-up, he thinks – the house, finance, and the help the Dean can get. Would there be any chance of having a secret 'look-round', he asked? In the circumstances there was in fact little chance. The whole affair was still strictly confidential and not even the Deanery could be inspected. In the event, a mutually-agreeable compromise was reached. The Jaspers travelled incognito to York, lunched with Stuart and Brenda Blanch, and then afterwards, on their way home they made 'a quick recce from the City Wall' of the Deanery.[6] Hardly a satisfactory solution, but on the basis of it Ronald wrote to the Prime Minister accepting his kind offer to recommend to the Queen his appointment as Dean of York.

RETURN TO THE NORTH

The service of installation was held on Friday 10 October 1975 in a crowded Minster. These occasions had been acquiring more 'pomp and ceremony' down the years. (In 1858 Augustus Duncombe had been installed as Dean by the acting sub-chanter immediately after Matins on a Saturday morning.)[7]

It was a lovely sunny autumn day for the installation and the new Dean was surrounded by friends from near and far, not least his colleagues from the Liturgical Commission, all enjoying a break from battles raging at the time to have the new services accepted. Ronald preached about worship and the need to draw from tradition – but also to discover new ways forward in the liturgy.

The Jaspers were happy to be in York. Ronald wrote: 'It has been a joy for my wife and me to come to York. My wife is a North-countrywoman by birth, and I regard myself as a Northcountryman by adoption, having worked in the North-East for some 20 years. So for us it has been a homecoming: and we have been deeply touched by the warmth of the welcome we have received.'

David, the Jaspers' son, was ordained just after they went to York in 1976, and in October 1977 Ronald conducted David's wedding service. Their daughter Christine had married a priest – Nicholas Reade. Writing to a friend at Christmas 1977 Ronald wondered if he and Betty were unique, 'Our Son, Daughter, son-in-law and daughter-in-law are all Honours graduates in theology and both men are ordained, Betty is thankful that she has her feet firmly on the ground with a degree in Domestic Science.' While working for his doctorate at Durham University, David spent a short period as curate of St Oswald's Durham, nearly forty years after his parents had been married in the church.

Ronald always enjoyed his visits to Christine and Nicholas's parishes. He felt a particular kinship with Nicholas who was also Mirfield-trained, and he first learned the skills of a grandparent with their daughter Claire. Later he enjoyed his times with his grandchildren in Durham. He was very proud of David's academic achievements.

Making changes at the Minster

Not surprisingly, there were things which the new Dean wished to change, and as always there were those who accepted his ideas gladly and willingly, those who accepted them reluctantly, and some who could only accept them unwillingly. An early misunderstanding arose out of the difference between the York statutes and the way things were done at Westminster Abbey. A certain amount of confusion might be thought to exist at the Abbey, because Queen Elizabeth I's signature is lacking on the Abbey statutes. Because of the doubtful authority of this foundation document, much is done there 'according to custom', but it has never been doubted that the Dean of Westminster is the 'Ordinary' within the Abbey. That is to say, that the ordering of the services is his prerogative, however much (or little) he may choose to consult with his capitular colleagues. Ronald started to act as if a similar situation existed at York, until it was pointed out that this was not the case. True, he was *primus inter pares*, but Deans of York (like his decanal colleagues in many other cathedrals) need to act according to that more broadly democratic concept.

Since 1926, under Dean Norris, there had been a sung Eucharist each Sunday in the Minster, but there was also still sung Matins at 11.00 a.m. Ronald wished to move the sung Eucharist to this time and make it the centrepiece of the morning worship. Furthermore, he wanted this service to be held in the nave rather than in the choir at the high altar. Many if not most of those who made up the regular Sunday congregation at the Minster were sympathetic to the changes, and Ronald was supported by the York Chapter. True to his democratic principles Ronald decided to explain to the Minster congregation the liturgical and pastoral principles behind these proposals. After all, he had spent many years performing such a task up and down the country. For some reason, no one is now quite sure why, things did not go according to plan and the meeting ended discordantly, with Ronald clearly displaying his displeasure. There were no further congregational meetings during his time at York.

A member of the Minster congregation tells that one of the results of this confrontation was that Ronald became unpopular with a small group of 'die-hards' and this sometimes made him appear abrupt. In fact he was deeply hurt by the whole struggle, and 'kept to his guns' only because he believed that it was vitally important for the life of the Minster that the worship should be enlivened, changed and reformed. The reward for his efforts was soon seen in a huge increase in the Sunday congregations, and the praise poured on the service and its setting by thousands and thousands of visitors. The new worship also attracted new members of the congregation, although Ronald never wanted to poach from other churches.

Here we might explore the impression that the new Dean made upon those he worked among in York. We have to remember that during his first four years, that is until the publication of the ASB in 1980, he was carrying an enormous double burden. He needed to travel to London at least once a week, sometimes twice; the correspondence continued unabated; he was in constant touch with Derek Pattinson and the General Synod office in Church House, with the secretary to the Commission (Barbara Ebdale who had succeeded the long-serving Daphne Fraser and later Pamela Aldwinckle), in fact with all those who were now concerned with the essentially practical details of producing the book.

Alongside this was the task of getting to know not just the Minster – but York. The Dean of York has a very definite civic role. One of those with whom Ronald worked closely, Dr John Shannon, secretary of the York Civic Trust, is of the opinion that Ronald was quite clear on the direction he wished to go in York. He had a particular task which he had to complete for the Church of England, and, as he had told the Archbishop of York, he intended to see it through to the final stages. But he would not allow this to interfere with what he believed were his duties in York, about which he was quite decisive and positive, Dr Shannon says.

It may be that feathers were ruffled occasionally, but that is the price of firm leadership. And he would be his own man; at the first meeting of the Friends of York Minster he told them that his name was neither Milner-White nor Alan Richardson (whatever admiration he had for both of them). He held the *office* of Dean of York in high regard, and thought that others should. It was not 'Dean Jasper' that needed to be deferred to, he was but one of the long line of those who had occupied the office, but the dignity of the Dean of York.

Among his colleagues and associates, as well as those who were hierarchically responsible to him, were some who felt that Ronald took this responsibility for the dignity of the office too seriously. The result was that the brisk, efficient, decisive man of affairs contrasted with the much warmer, amusing and friendly person which some knew was only just below the surface. A regular worshipper at York commented, 'He could appear cold, but those who thought so never looked up to see the twinkle in his eyes.' Inevitably there were those who never penetrated the protective screen – and that was a pity.

Of one thing all his colleagues at York are in complete agreement – the warmth of the hospitality in the Deanery. Canon Raymond Hockley tells how when he first arrived in December 1976 the Jaspers were kindness itself. 'I was invited to dinner on Christmas Day and immediately felt at ease with Ronald and Betty. He was fun, hospitable and considerate; and so was Betty. The parties were full of gentle laughter.' Canon Hockley goes on, 'I had known Ronald only as a Chairman of many Committees but discovered that he was a lovable man. He and Betty were as though they were still on their honeymoon. They were obviously devoted to each other (walking through Dean's Park holding hands together) and the Deanery was a real home.'

Jean Mayland, who had worked with Ronald for a number of years as a member of the Liturgical Commisssion, went to York in 1982, when her husband Ralph became a canon of York. She also tells of happy times in the Deanery. 'When entertaining in his own home with Betty his warmth came through. They regularly entertained the Canons and their families. He always looked after the Minster during August so that Canons with families could go on holiday. When we came back we would be entertained to supper to tell them all about it and then Ronald and Betty themselves would go away when the school holidays were over. Ronald and Betty began the Workman's Party at Christmas. In their day it really was a workman's party and all the stoneyard staff came and the Canons and wives helped to "wait on". Having children and grandchildren of his own Ronald got on well with our younger daughter Alex.'

REORDERING OF THE NAVE

As Dean of York Ronald Jasper was not narrow in his aims. His reputation as a liturgist had obviously gone before him, and no one could have been surprised that he would wish to apply at York the liturgical principles which he so firmly held. Although some of the changes were not always fully understood, as we have seen, he believed that he was building on the already-existing and widely-acknowledged high standards and dignity of the Minster's worship. This could be further improved in one particular way, he thought. Not only should the principal Sunday Eucharist take place in the nave, but also many important diocesan, civic, and provincial occasions. Notable in the last category were the regular consecrations of bishops for the northern province, set in the context of the Eucharist. Always well attended, these also should be in the nave of the Minster, Ronald argued. Nothing irritates a congregation more than not being able to see what is going on. Ronald had given thought during his work on the Commission – and encouraged others to do so – to the presentation of the Eucharist. Good liturgy needs to be both visible and audible, 'done in the face of all people'. To this end Ronald worked with the Minster surveyor, Charles

Brown, on a re-ordering of the nave that would provide maximum visibility and audibility for both the Minster's regular worship and also for the grander 'set pieces'. It would certainly be fair to say that the resulting re-ordering of the furniture was not without its critics, and both friend and foe quickly dubbed it 'Mount Jasper'. Yet the truth of the matter is that it did achieve its objective, and the worship in the nave of York Minster did become more accessible to a far greater degree than ever before. In 1995 'Mount Jasper' was demolished, but the principle of the Eucharist in the Nave remains.

REMOVAL OF TRAFFIC

Another York project to which Ronald gave a good deal of time and energy was the pedestrianization of Deangate. The Esher report in 1969 had recommended the closing of this road, which runs down the south side of the Minster within feet of the Cathedral wall, in order to help preserve the character of the city. Equally, it would be of considerable environmental advantage to the fabric of the Minster if there were no longer 10,000 vehicles a day passing within two yards of the south-west tower.[8] Dr Shannon of the York Civic Trust took an early opportunity to share his feelings on the matter with the newly arrived Dean in 1968, who quickly took up the matter. He arranged a meeting in the Deanery, to which he personally invited the appropriate municipal authorities and pressed them for action. It was a long-drawn-out affair, and not until 1989 could John Southgate, Ronald's successor, take a well-publicized lunch in the middle of a traffic-free Deangate.[9]

For many years St William's College, at the east end of the Minster in College Street, was something of a millstone round the neck of the Diocese of York, until the Dean and Chapter took it on and became its Trustees.[10] During their time in York Ronald and Betty set about launching a St William's College appeal, which was successful. The portrait-style photographs of both Ronald and Betty which are to be seen in the Bishops' Chamber in the college, were regarded by both of them as a fitting place for a commemoration of all their work in York. The college became the venue for coffee for the congregation after the Sunday morning Eucharist. It was always well patronized and provided an opportunity for the congregation to meet the clergy and other members of the Minster staff. Canon Ralph Mayland recalls, 'Ronald valued this "exposure".'

Canon Mayland provides a pleasant anecdote which, he says, typifies the warmth and care of Ronald's decanal ministry.

> When Ronald saw me after my hour and a half interview with Archbishop Blanch about my going to York as a Residentiary Canon I said on taking my leave, in jest, that I couldn't come unless my goat could come too. Ronald telephoned a day later to say he had consulted the City Fathers as to whether or not there was a by-law about animals and, because there was not, it would be all right for me to bring the goat! A sequel was that both Ronald and Betty attended the birth of her kid, born immediately after the Palm Sunday Eucharist and thus named Hosanna. She lived to a ripe eleven years and enjoyed many hours browsing on the herbs and grass in the Deanery garden, by kind and welcome permission of the Dean – and to become the fan of countless photographers.

'Mount Jasper', the closing of Deangate, and the extensive renovation of St William's College are but high-profile examples of Ronald's work in York, but there were many other events, occasions and projects of significance and importance during his occupation of the Deanery.

Because of his great interest in W. H. Frere, he was particularly interested in the celebrations to commemorate the fiftieth anniversary of the 'Malines Conversations'. There had been an attempt in the 1920s to build a theological bridge between the Church of England and the Roman Catholic Church. Frere was among the Anglican scholars who took part, but the inspiration for the conversations came from Lord Halifax, whose family had long connections with the Minster. During the 1976 celebrations, Cardinal Suenens of Malines decorated Ronald with the Croix D'Or de Saint Rombayt. In 1987 there was a series of splendid occasions to commemorate the 1350th anniversary of the foundation of the Minster in AD 627. A great service was held on Easter Eve that year with the Archbishop present; there was a Children's Day; a special musical celebration of the Eucharist on St Peter's Day; and a concert in the autumn of the year given by the Royal Liverpool Philharmonic Orchestra.

The next year saw the Golden Jubilee of the Friends of York Minster (one of the oldest and most vigorous of similar cathedral organizations), which was an event marked by the complete renovation and refurbishment of the Zouche Chapel, and a visit by the Queen Mother, the Friends' Patron. The furnishing of the Minster crypt, parts of which had been revealed during a restoration in 1972, was completed with the provision of three most attractive altars commemorating St Hilda, St Paulinus and King Edwin. Then there were comings and goings; notably the retirement of Dr Francis Jackson, organist and Master of the Music since 1946 who had been associated with the Minster as man and boy for over fifty years. Then in 1983 came the retirement of Dr Stuart Blanch as Archbishop of York.

Throughout 1981–2 Archbishop Blanch conducted a 'Visitation of the Minster' – the first since the days of Archbishop Temple fifty years earlier. It was an important moment in the history of the Minster, Ronald thought.

> It was no light task, and it was certainly time-consuming. To the man in the street it could be regarded as of little moment: but the Visitation Articles drove us all to examine every aspect of our life in the minutest detail. A complete assessment will take time: but already we have felt the benefit of the exercise and improvements have been instituted. Without the Archbishop's probing mind this would not have been done; and taking a long view, I believe the Visitation may well prove to be significant in the history of the Minster.[11]

Now there was to be a new Archbishop. The choice of Dr John Habgood, Bishop of Durham, was no great surprise. His experience, ability, intellectual gifts and theological expertise had long marked him out for high office. He was enthroned in the Minster on 18 November 1983 at a service which was unique in two ways: it was televised in full and the Prime Minister (Margaret Thatcher) attended at her own request.

Retirement

Archbishop Habgood and Ronald worked alongside each other for less than twelve months for Ronald had decided that he would retire in the summer of 1984, when he would be sixty-seven. Although they did not have a long time together in York, they were well-known to each other through the General Synod, and in particular through the Archbishop's chairmanship of the ASB working party.

Archbishop Habgood has written of Ronald, 'Our subsequent collaboration in York was all too short as he was already well on the road to retirement by the time I arrived.'

Just before Ronald left York the General Synod had one of its regular summer sessions at the University of York. On Sunday 8 July 1984 the members and staff of the Synod attended the Eucharist in the Minster. One member of Synod recalls, 'The Minster was packed and looked immaculate. Ronald who had done so much to complete the restoration and tidy, beautify and reorder the building must have thought that he was going to retire and leave it in perfect order. The Archbishop of York made a short and gracious comment about Ronald's retirement in his sermon. Ronald bowed in response. The service was very wonderful, a high level of presentation and worship drawing on new and old.'

DRAMATIC CONCLUSION

Few ministries, let alone that of a dean, have ended in such a way as that of Ronald Jasper at York! During the night of 9 July 1984 a lightning bolt struck the Minster; the roof of the south transept was destroyed and the rest of the Cathedral was saved only by the skill and courage of firemen. One of the results of the damage was to create a huge question mark over the safety of the south transept gable, with its famous Rose Window and beautiful sixteenth-century glass. It was standing unsupported by the roof timbers which normally gave it strength.

Summoned from his bed, the Dean took part in the hasty evacuation of many precious and valuable items from the Minster. It was a risky business, but for a time no one could guess how far the fire might travel, added to which was the danger of valuable objects being irreparably damaged by the necessary gallons of water being poured on the Minster roof. It was a terrible experience for someone who had come to love and care for the Minster, far above any of the necessities of office or duty.

Almost immediately there was a good deal of silly and stupid speculation about the cause of the fire. The thunderbolt, it was suggested, was a direct intervention by God in protest against the consecration in the Minster, a few weeks earlier, of David Jenkins as Bishop of Durham. Bishop Jenkins was a person known for his liberal interpretation of both scripture and doctrine, and the victim of an ill-informed and ridiculous press campaign.

These fanciful theories received short shrift from the Dean of York in his final address to the Minster staff on 15 July. It gave him the opportunity to make a strong declaration about his belief in the providence of God.

> Should God constantly intervene and disrupt the normal course of nature, simply to save men from pain and disaster? What kind of world would it become if the law of gravity suddenly became inoperative if a particular person had unfortunately fallen over a cliff? If God were to intervene in ways such as this, he would have to do it for all and sundry and indeed suspend the laws of nature, otherwise he would be acting arbitrarily and unfairly. Or what kind of world would it be like with no laws of nature? Or if we were never sure that they were going to operate or not? Not only would it mean a chaotic world and an arbitrary God. It would also mean that we would lose our freedom and responsibility of action. There would be no need for us to bother about anyone or anything – God would be looking after it all. We live in a world where by the very nature of things, opposites can happen – success and failure, brilliant achievement and tragic disaster, happiness and sorrow. Yet these opposites can have a strange kind of relationship. If we are to set any store by such things as love, courage, goodness, sacrifice we simply must have a world like ours, with its problems and difficulties, for them to exist. And if we are prepared to accept the world as we find it, we can accept a God who acts consistently and who gives us freedom – freedom to do and accept His will, or freedom to reject him and have nothing to do with him.

As he continued, he applied these sound theological principles to the sad happenings at York. He told those who had, like himself, wept tears as they saw the result of the fire: 'That simply is how I see things, and nothing that has happened in these last few days – my final days at the Minster – has given me any cause to have my convictions shaken. I still believe that God loves this place and that I can turn to him as my loving Father as long as I do my best to seek and fulfil His will.' Then he thanked them all for their devotion. He particularly thanked the firemen and the police, as well as the Minster staff and the local firms, who had helped in so many ways in the preceding hectic days. 'The response has been overwhelming: it has encouraged us enormously: and it has revealed a great depth of kindness and love. That love is God's love. Indeed, during this past week it has never once occurred to me that God has been unheeding, unkind or even angry. On the contrary I remain firmly convinced that God loves this place, that he loves me, and that he loves all his children.'

There remained only for the Dean to say 'goodbye'. He said it had been suggested that he should stay on to 'see things through' but, he said, having thought deeply about it, he was clear that would be wrong. He told them: 'In the first place the constitutional processes of finding my successor are already under way: and any attempt on my part to delay them or put them into reverse would only create confusion. A long and difficult job faces the new Dean: the sooner he comes the better; and in the long run I would not be serving the Minster's best interests by hanging around and delaying his arrival. Meanwhile, until he comes, I am ready to help in any way possible.' It was a sad way to go, but he was not unaware of God's continuing love: 'After 44 years therefore, as parish priest, university teacher, Canon of Westminster and Dean of York, I step down, thankful for God's many mercies in a very varied ministry. God has shown his love for me in a host of different ways. And I can repay that love by continuing to serve him as best I can in the years to come with those gifts He has chosen to give me.'

Sadly those years were fewer than Ronald might have reasonably expected, and certainly fewer than either his family and friends had hoped.

NOTES

1. Adrian Hastings, *A History of English Christianity 1920–1985*, London, 1986, pp. 606–9.
2. Borthwick Library, Bishopthorpe Papers, York, BP2/DIOC/1.2/2.
3. Bishopthorpe Papers, BP2/DIOC/1.2/2.
4. Westminster Abbey Muniments DF 54.
5. Bishopthorpe Papers, BP2/DIOC/1.2/2. (Dr Blanch was wrong in saying that Jasper had been 'brought up' in the North of England, but correct in saying he had been educated and served in the ministry there.)
6. Bishopthorpe Papers, BP2/DIOC/1.2/2.
7. Friends of York Minster 51st Annual Report, 1980, p. 19.

8. York Civic Trust Annual Report for 1968–69, p. 2.
9. York Civic Trust Annual Report for 1988–89, photo between pp. 32–33.
10. G. E. Aylmer and Reginald Cant (eds), *A History of York Minster*, Oxford, 1977, pp. 97–8 and 557–8.
11. Friends of York Minster 54th Annual Report, 1983, p. 2.

10

RETIREMENT IN RIPON

RONALD HAD LONG been of the opinion that he ought to retire when he reached the age of sixty-seven. By the present day retirement rules for Church of England clergy, a pension is available from the age of sixty-five, but the exact point between then and their seventieth birthday is left to the discretion of each individual. It seemed to Ronald that almost ten years at York would be about right. This decision meant that, in circumstances Ronald could never have anticipated, a new dean could be appointed to tackle the aftermath of the Minster fire.

The Jaspers were keen to remain in the north of England; they both felt most comfortable there. The choice of Ripon afforded them a number of benefits: a busy market town with easily available facilities; good access to the national motorway system; and proximity to the countryside of the Yorkshire Dales which they both loved. Additionally, there was the cathedral. After years worshipping in Exeter Cathedral, Westminster Abbey and York Minster, a similar type of church on the doorstep would be a great bonus, they believed, particularly as advancing years curtailed travel.

An early approach was made to the Bishop of Ripon who wrote in March 1983 to say that he had discussed the matter with the Dean and that he was 'enormously enthusiastic about your proposal to live in Ripon'. The Bishop went on, 'We hope that this would enable you to play a full part in the regular liturgical life of the Cathedral – your participation and advice would be enormously appreciated. We hope also that you would be willing to act as a consultant in liturgical matters generally within the Diocese.'

In the event Ronald performed few liturgical duties in the cathedral at Ripon. Canon Ronald McFadden, who was a residentiary canon at the time, recalls that when not doing duty elsewhere, Ronald was usually in the Cathedral congregation at the Parish Communion with Betty. Indeed, when she was 'on duty' making coffee after the service, Dr Jasper was to be discovered happily brewing, serving and washing up. In the judgement of Canon McFadden, Ronald's greatest contribution to the life of the cathedral during his retirement years was his lecturing in the Cathedral Study Centre. 'Over the years he covered quite a bit of the ground contained in *A Companion to the Alternative Service Book* and most of *The Development of the Anglican Liturgy 1662–1980*. His lectures alternated with Anthony Hanson's on the Bible. Those were epic years in the life of the Study Centre. He was very relaxed during his lectures and enjoyed the question time afterwards.'

One particular spell of duty elsewhere was between September 1988 and June 1989 when he undertook the interregnum at Masham. In that period Ronald took all the services (except for a few that his son David took when Ronald was not available), and he and Betty became very involved with the life of the parish some nine miles from Ripon. Dr David Smith, Director of the Borthwick Institute of Historical Research in the University of York, was one of the churchwardens at the time. He writes that Ronald: 'Made the difficult period of an interregnum run very smoothly and we were delighted that he and Betty took such an active interest in the parish. I believe that they both much enjoyed the visits to Masham and they made friends there. It was not just a matter of Sunday services and occasional weddings – Ronald was always on call for advice in matters ecclesiastical and administrative, and during Lent gave a splendid series of three lectures on Anglican liturgy since the Reformation, which are still very much remembered.'

On the appointment of their new vicar in 1989 the Masham parochial meeting wrote to Ronald saying how much they had appreciated his great support. 'We have needed your dedicated and practical approach. We shall miss you,' the secretary wrote.

The comment has already been made that Ronald shared with many of those concerned about standards of worship in the Church of England, an anxiety about the teaching of liturgy in theological colleges and ordination training schemes, and the apparent neglect of the subject of liturgy in the country's faculties of theology. The two matters were obviously related. If the universities were not producing the teachers then the colleges and courses would find it difficult, if not impossible, to recruit suitably qualified staff. And the circle was more vicious than that. If colleges were not teaching the subject neither were they enthusing students to take an academic interest in this area, which might have prompted some to take up post-graduate work in liturgy. Ronald had tried hard at King's in London to encourage those who showed an interest, and at the present time the fruits of those days are still apparent. His successor at King's, Geoffrey Cuming, was also a notable liturgical talent-spotter and encourager, but sadly the field remains small.

Back at Durham

In 1988 the University of Durham was experiencing considerable difficulty in maintaining the teaching of liturgy in the department of theology there. Fr Christopher Walsh, who had formerly helped in the department, had just left Ushaw leaving only Dr Anthony Gelston to teach in this field. David Jasper, Ronald's son, had moved to Durham as Principal of St Chad's College, and he suggested to Canon Daniel Hardy, the Van Mildert Professor of Divinity, that he should approach his father about the possibility of returning to Durham University – fifty years after he had left – in order to teach liturgy part-time. Canon Hardy wrote to Ronald: 'Since I am very anxious to build up the teaching of Liturgy in Durham in the years to come, it could be an enormous help and pleasure to have you here to teach. I hope you will consider it.' In view of his concern about the teaching of liturgy Ronald agreed to this, and travelled up to Durham for two years. His work there during that period was much appreciated. Dr Gelston made it very clear in a personal letter he wrote to Ronald in March 1990. 'I just want to express my personal very warm thanks for the teaching you have provided over the last two years, your ready help with examinations, and your generous help and advice over our plans for the future. We really are most grateful, and I do not know what we should have done without you.'

After a lifetime of 'giving a paper' up and down the country, Ronald was generous in allocating time to addressing the local retired clergy. There was a fellow-feeling for those who like himself had retired from the front line, but equally there was his continuing concern to teach and inform. He did not want them to be unaware of the latest in scholarly thinking nor of the current developments in liturgical reform. The notes taken by one retired priest of a talk given by Ronald in October 1987, record that he spoke to them of Gese's essay on 'The origin of the Lord's Supper' in his book *Zur Bithscen-Theologie*. There was no concession to easy-going, intellectually lazy days for the retired priests of Ripon while Dr Jasper was around! If they were being challenged to keep their minds actively ticking over it was by someone who had set himself two major tasks for his retirement. The first was the completion of *A Companion to the Alternative Service Book*. He had been working on this as joint author with Paul Bradshaw for some time.

Last writings

Just before leaving York in June 1984, Ronald received a letter from Judith Longman reminding him that the current contractual agreement with SPCK was that they would receive the manuscript by 31 December, that being twelve months later than the original date. Ronald wrote to Paul Bradshaw on 7 June saying, 'obviously after this month I shall be able to give more time to these things'. And indeed he did, and the book came out on time.

The *Companion* was the first of his two projects; the other was a quite different undertaking and one very close to his heart. Years earlier, Ronald had published a book in which he detailed all the proposals made for liturgical revision in the Church of England from 1662 onwards. Almost every one of these had proved abortive. And he had edited the correspondence of Walter Frere, which gives such a clear picture of the 1927–1928 liturgical débâcle. How was it that The Alternative Service Book had succeeded where others had failed? *The Development of Anglican Liturgy 1662–1980* was Ronald's explanation of this. (Incidentally, he had originally wanted it titled *Uniformity and Flexibility*.)

This was a story that needed telling, and there was no one better placed than Ronald Jasper to tell it in authoritative detail. To do so he would need to go over some of the ground he had already explored in his earlier books, but now was the opportunity to draw together that earlier material together with the work his friend Geoffrey Cuming had done in *A History of Anglican Liturgy*, the second edition of which appeared in 1982. The new information which Ronald's book contained is a detailed account of the process of liturgical revision in England, from the formation of the Liturgical Commission in 1955 to the publication of the ASB in 1980. Since Ronald was involved at every stage of this process, there was never any danger that the account would not be correct down to the last detail. The only other person who had given similar exacting attention to these matters, Colin Buchanan, adjudged that Ronald had picked 'a most careful (and beautifully exact) course through the thick jungle of interlocking influences and competing materials'. Buchanan believed it to be Ronald's *magnum opus*.

The Development is a book of immense detail; perhaps a little daunting for the non-specialist, nevertheless of great merit as autobiography. Indeed, this biographer has already admitted he has been both stimulated and daunted by those autobiographical sections; not wanting to repeat the account that Ronald supplies there, but also very ready to acknowledge the immense value to his own work of its availability. What the book lacks, and rightly so, is an assessment of his personal contribution to this great piece of work for Christ and the Kingdom. That he was about a task of the greatest importance Ronald had no doubt; for he was acutely aware of the need for worship which was both inspirational and intellectually respectable. His modesty lay in his assessment of the importance of his own contribution to the task.

Ronald Jasper, we have noted, never made any claims to be an original liturgical scholar. He saw himself primarily as a church historian who had come to specialize in this field. Nor had he any pretentions to being a skilled writer of either poetry or prose, yet he could write lucidly and clearly and had a good ear for a telling phrase. In the particular field of literary composition, he was anxious to draw upon the skills of gifted practitioners.

Companions in the task

This willingness to harness the gifts of others was what made Ronald such an ideal chairman of the Commission. It did not always make for less work for himself; the efforts of such diverse groups of experts needed a skilled ringmaster. But neither was he ever jealous of the expertise of others; in fact he always wished to give them their head. In the field of liturgical theology there were two people in particular on whom he relied and trusted explicitly. That they also gave him their friendship was a bonus. No biographer of Ronald Jasper, no account of the heady and hectic days of the detailed work on the ASB could omit the most honourable mention of their names, even though both have been mentioned a number of times: Geoffrey Cuming and Charles Whitaker.

The sad fact is that all three – Geoffrey, Charles and Ronald – having been born within months of each other, also died within a space of two years of each other; Charles and Geoffrey only days apart. Charles Whitaker died suddenly on 21 March 1988 in his native Cumbria, and Geoffrey Cuming died three days later in Houston, Texas following heart surgery which had apparently gone successfully, but which his general constitution was unable to withstand.

Ronald gave the address at Charles's funeral held in the Parish Church of St Cuthbert, Kirkby Ireleth where he had previously been vicar for seventeen years. It was to this remote country parish that the summons had come in 1965 for its scholar-parson to join the Liturgical Commission. Few of his parishioners knew that their vicar was a liturgical scholar of international renown. They were perhaps surprised to hear the former chairman of the Liturgical Commission, and recently retired Dean of York, saying:

> Charles was one of an all-too-rare breed – once one of the glories of the Church of England, but now in the changed conditions of today sadly so seldom encountered – the country parson cum scholar. As an authority on Christian Initiation Charles had an international reputation: and of the six books he wrote – mostly on that subject – I was pleased to have a hand in most, either by asking him to write them or by being in some measure responsible for their publication. It was small wonder, therefore, that in 1965 he was asked to join the Liturgical Commission, which he served faithfully for some fifteen years, becoming one of the principle architects of The Alternative Service Book. The Baptism and Confirmation services were entirely his, as were the Calendar and Lectionary, the seasonal Blessings, and much of the Intercessions: and in those last hectic years in the final run-up to publication, he was always there to help if proofs needed checking or some piece of information were urgently required.

What made this scholar different, said Ronald, was the fact that he rarely left his study for the conference-hall or lecture room, which were not his scene; he preferred the quiet of his study in his country vicarage. Ronald told the congregation:

> He was happy in his ministry here because at heart he was a countryman. He loved the beauty of the fells and the riches they had to offer – witness the books of superb photographs of wild flowers taken in

> retirement. But he loved the people here too – a love shown not only in his pastoral work. It was also shown in his interest in a variety of good causes – conservation, nursing, local government, campanology, and in his willingness to serve the community. I wonder how many of you know that years ago in one of his parishes he acted as the postman: and in those far-off days when the post still came on Christmas Day, it was his great delight both to take the services in Church and to deliver the cards and parcels to the parish, providing him with an opportunity of wishing everyone personally a very happy Christmas.

Geoffrey Cuming was cast in a different mould. In the tribute he contributed to the *Church Times*, Ronald called him, 'A genial giant, he loved travel and was drawn more to academic life, having spells of teaching in Durham, London and Cuddesdon in a ministry that was largely parochial. His circle of friends was wide; he encouraged the younger scholar; and in retirement he found particular delight in teaching theological students for several months each year in Berkeley, California. It was all done despite considerable physical disabilities incurred during the war.' Of Geoffrey it was said that no one hesitated to ask him a question lest in the asking the inquirer might be made to feel a fool for not knowing the answer; information was shared freely and generously with the enthusiasm of a teacher whose primary concern is to arouse a corresponding enthusiasm in his pupil. There is a whole generation of liturgical scholars in England who would want to acknowledge the encouragement and sheer practical help that Geoffrey Cuming gave them in pursuing their researches and studies. Or as Colin Buchanan said during the memorial service held at St Peter's Wolvercote, 'There were many in his lifetime to compare him, with especial weight upon the adjective, to the judicious Dr Hooker. That was Geoffrey indeed. But because his spirituality and emotions were private, and his liturgical expertise and creativity very public, it is inevitable that a tribute to him should make much of his work. I hope that will be pardoned. It in no way ignores the awareness of a warm, living and vulnerable person who stood behind all the work, and poured himself into it.'

Summing up, Ronald said that Charles and Geoffrey were a wonderful, learned pair carrying their scholarship lightly: delightful companions, diligent and devout pastors; two great sons of Anglicanism.

There is no reason to believe that the sudden and unexpected loss of these former colleagues gave Ronald any more than those regular 'intimations of mortality' to which we are all subject in later life, as friends and relations depart from the earthly scene. He had suffered from a bad back for a number of years, in fact it was this problem which caused his single absence from meetings of the Liturgical Commission over all his years of membership. In January 1986 he spent a fortnight in hospital and then in late September 1989, he went into hospital again. In a letter to Lord Coggan he said, 'A bug caught on holiday in Scotland as long ago as mid-summer served me rather badly and we have had a miserable few months, culminating in an operation. But the ending is happy. I have been cleared on all counts and I am feeling better than I have been for the past four years. So we are delighted and feel that the discomfort has not been in vain. But enough of our problems.'

The last days

Unfortunately the 'bug' did not go away and in April 1990 he was admitted to Harrogate hospital once again. The planned operation was comparatively minor, but he suddenly went into heart failure and died on 11 April 1990, Maundy Thursday – the day of the institution of the Lord's Supper. Surely that is a poignant fact when we recall his lifelong concern for the dignity and rightful celebration of the Holy Eucharist.

We have two accounts of his last days: one from a former colleague at York Minster, and one from his newer friends at Ripon Cathedral. Canon Ronald McFadden went to see him. 'I saw him last on Palm Sunday in hospital – I was on my way to Norwich to conduct Holy Week – he was in an extremely happy mood and he said so: "content and expectant". I used the Passiontide blessing from the ASB: "Christ crucified draw you to Himself, so that you find in Him a sure ground for faith, a firm support for hope, and the assurance of sins forgiven etc" – I felt his smile as I slipped away expressed gratitude for words from the book to which he gave so much and which gave so much to him.'

Canon Ralph Mayland tells of visiting him in those last days, and of how Ronald told him that he regarded York as being the pinnacle of his career. Later Canon Mayland ministered to him at the last:

anointing him and giving the holy sacrament of the Body and Blood of Christ for the last time.

The funeral was held in York Minster on 18 April. The previous evening Ralph Mayland had received his body into the Minster where it rested overnight. The service was conducted by the Dean, Canon Raymond Hockley and Canon Mayland. The committal was at York crematorium. On 1 June Dr David Jasper, assisted by Ronald's son-in-law the Revd Nicholas Reade, laid his ashes to rest by the altar of the Minster's Zouche Chapel, the restoration of which Ronald had so lovingly overseen while Dean. The next day saw a memorial Eucharist at York Minster, into which memories and echoes of Ronald's whole ministry were incorporated. The hymn for the entry, 'Christ is made a sure foundation', was sung to the tune known as 'Westminster Abbey' because it derives from the alleluias at the end of Purcell's anthem 'O God thou art my God, early will I seek thee'. (Purcell was organist and Master of the Choristers at the Abbey from 1679 to 1695.) The Dean of York, John Southgate, read the Gospel. Jean Mayland, who had served on the Liturgical Commission under Ronald, led the intercessions, and the Offertory hymn 'Father, Lord of all creation' was sung to the stirring tune 'Abbot's Leigh', composed by another Liturgical Commission colleague and friend Cyril Taylor; while the anthem 'We wait for thy loving kindness, O God' was a combination of words selected by Cyril Armitage (Precentor of Westminster Abbey 1933–51), and music by another former Abbey organist William McKie (1941–63). One of the features of the service was the playing of Vaughan Williams *The Lark Ascending*, at Ronald's particular request, after the peace. The Archbishop of York (John Habgood) presided (no other verb would have been right on this occasion), and the former Archbishop, Stuart Blanch, preached the sermon.

In that address Dr Blanch said, 'God was the strength of his being. Ronald was a strong man, of steadfast purpose and remarkable stamina. To some of his pupils he must have seemed a formidable man, but for me he was an unfailing friend, with whom it was a pleasure to share a visit to Harry Ramsden's Fish Restaurant. But his strength was not the strength that flowed from rude health or an iron constitution, it was the strength that God supplied.'

The final choral music was no more, and certainly no less, than that which had concluded every Sunday Eucharist throughout Ronald's time at the Minster: the unaccompanied singing by the choir in procession of Psalm 150, with the concluding 'Gloria', echoing around the south transept to such telling effect.

In his funeral address at Kirkby Ireleth just over two years earlier, Ronald had said of Charles Whitaker: 'That eminent Churchman, Cardinal Suenens, was fond of speaking of "the surprises of the Spirit" – the way in which God worked through what people would often regard as coincidence or chance. I like to think of Charles as one of the surprises of the Spirit. God put him, endowed with just the right gifts to live in just the right place in order to do just the right job just when it was needed.' How equally true it would be to apply such an epitaph to Ronald Jasper.

Neither proud parents, nor any caring parish priest in Plymouth sixty years beforehand, could have guessed that the destiny of this young ordinand was that of being instrumental in bringing about such profound changes in the worship of the Church of England. Even later at Mirfield, and in those early parishes in the diocese of Durham, there was not the slightest indication of the importance of his future life's work. Yet with the blessed benefit of hindsight, we can discern at each stage the preparations that were being made: through his pastoral work, in his academic study and research, and through his growing ecumenical awareness. Even so, there is one other thing: over and above everything else Ronald had a profound concern for the high dignity and purpose of Christian worship. So that at every time, and in every place, it might be worthy of God in Trinity; Father, Son, and Holy Spirit.

RONALD JASPER: PUBLISHED WRITINGS

BOOKS

1954 *Prayer Book Revision in England 1800–1900*. London, SPCK.
Walter Howard Frere: his Correspondence on Liturgical Revision and Construction, Alcuin Club Collections no. XXXIX. London, SPCK.
1959 *The Position of the Celebrant at the Eucharist*, Alcuin Club Pamphlet no. XVI. London, Mowbray.
1960 *Arthur Cayley Headlam: Life and Letters of a Bishop*. London, Faith Press.
n.d.('Early 1960s' P. J. Jagger, *The Alcuin Club: An Annotated Bibliography*, 1975, p. 48), *The Canon*, Alcuin Worship Today Pamphlets, Alcuin Club.
1963 *The Search for an Apostolic Liturgy*, Alcuin Club Pamphlet no. XVIII. London, Mowbray.
1965 *The Renewal of Worship* (editor and contributor). London, Oxford University Press.
1967 *George Bell, Bishop of Chichester*. London, Oxford University Press.
The Calendar and Lectionary (editor). London, Oxford University Press.
1968 *The Daily Office* (editor). London, SPCK and Epworth Press.
1970 *Some Aspects of the Liturgy in Contemporary Society*, Drawbridge Memorial Lecture 1970. London, Christian Evidence Society.
1971 *Holy Week Services* (editor). London, SPCK and Epworth Press.
1972 *A Christian's Prayer Book* (with Peter Coughlan and Teresa Rodrigues). London, Geoffrey Chapman.
Initiation and Eucharist (editor). London, SPCK.
1974 *The Eucharist Today: Studies in Series 3* (editor and contributor). London, SPCK.
1975 *An der Schwelle zum Gespaltenen Europa* (editor with E. Bethge). Stuttgart and Berlin, Kreuz Verlag.
Prayers of the Eucharist: Early and Reformed (with G. J. Cuming). London, Collins.
Worship and the Child (editor). London, SPCK.
1976 *Pray every Day* (with Peter Coughlan and David Jasper). London, Collins.
1978 *The Daily Office Revised* (editor). London, SPCK.
Every Day Pray (with Peter Coughlan and David Jasper) [US version of *Pray every Day*]. New York, Pueblo.
1980 *The Alternative Service Book: A Commentary by the Liturgical Commission* (editor). London, CIO Publishing.

Prayers of the Eucharist: Early and Reformed, 2nd enlarged edition (with G. J. Cuming). New York, Oxford University Press.

1982 *Getting the Liturgy Right* (editor and contributor). London, SPCK.

1986 *A Companion to the Alternative Service Book* (with P. F. Bradshaw). London, SPCK.

1987 *Herbert Newall Bate: a Reticent Genius*. York, Dean and Chapter of York.

Prayers of the Eucharist: Early and Reformed, 3rd enlarged edition (with G. J. Cuming). New York, Pueblo.

1989 *The Development of Anglican Liturgy 1662–1980*. London, SPCK.

1990 *Language and the Worship of the Church* (editor with David Jasper). London, Macmillan.

ARTICLES

1941 'A Note on Sir John Trevor', in *The Bulletin of the Institute of Historical Research*, vol. 18, p. 136.

1943 'Edward Eliot and the Acquisition of Grampound', in *The English Historical Review*, vol. LVIII, pp, 475–81.

1954 'Some notes on the Early Life of Bishop John Cosin', in *The Bishopric*, vol. 30, pp. 5–9.

1958 'Walter Howard Frere, Bishop, Religious, Scholar: A Memoir', in *Church Times*, 28 March, p. 10.

1960 'Arthur Cayley Headlam', in *The Church Quarterly Review*, vol. CLXI, pp. 308–17.

1965 'Gore on Liturgical Revision', in *The Church Quarterly Review*, vol. CLXVI, pp. 21–36.

'Ecumenical Liturgy', in *The Church Service Society Annual*, no. 35, pp. 44–56.

'The Language of Worship', in *The Reader*, vol. LXII, no. 11, pp. 205–208.

1968 'The Church Quarterly Review 1875–1968', in *The Church Quarterly*, vol. 1, pp. 136–41.

1969 'Liturgical Language in the Church of England', in *Societas Liturgica Papers*, no. 2.

1970 'The Gospel and the Sacraments: the Anglican Tradition', in *Oecumenica*, 1970, pp. 240–55.

'The Prayer Book in the Victorian Era', in *The Victorian Crisis of Faith* (ed. A Symondson), pp. 107–21. London, SPCK.

1971 'Liturgical Revision in the Church of England Today', in *Worship and Preaching*, vol. 2, pp. 24–8.

1972 'Holy Communion, Series 3', in *Church Music*, April 1972, pp. 11–12.

'Ecumenical Liturgy', in *One in Christ*, 1972, pp. 377–83.

Articles on Anglican Worship; Canon; Liturgics, Patristic; Ordination, Anglican; Procession, in *A Dictionary of Liturgy and Worship* (ed. J. G. Davies). London, SCM Press.

'We beheld his Glory', in *OHP Annual Review*, pp. 4–6.

1973 'Liturgy in the Anglican Communion 1968–73', in *Partners in Mission*, Report of the Anglican Consultative Council, pp. 70–86.

1974 'Penance in the Eucharist', in *Christian Celebration*, Winter, pp. 12–13.

1975 'Reconciliation: the Anglican Tradition', in *Music and Liturgy*, vol. 1, pp. 167–70.

'Religious Dance in England', in *Worship and Dance* (ed. J. G. Davies), pp. 22–8.

'A New Anglican Service Book', in *The Ampleforth Review*, pp. 87–90.

1976 'The Methodist Service Book 1975', in *The Epworth Review*, vol. 3, pp. 54–5.

'All Change', in *Mowbrays Journal*, no. 103, Spring, pp. 3–5.

1977 'Christian Initiation: the Anglican Position', in *Studia Liturgica*, vol. 12, pp. 116–25.

1983 'The Liturgical Movement', in *A New Dictionary of Christian Theology* (eds. A. Richardson and J. Bowden), pp. 335–6. London, SCM Press.

1984 'Growing Convergence in Liturgical Renewal: the Ecumenical Dimension', in *Liturgy*, vol. 8, pp. 194–201.

1985 'Liturgical Prayer: Another Look at the Lord's Prayer', in *The Crossroads*, Lent 1985, pp. 17–31.

1986 Articles on Anglican Worship; Canon; Liturgies, Patristic; Ordination, Anglican: Procession; Remembrance Sunday; Liturgical Revisions, in *A New Dictionary of Liturgy and Worship* (ed. J. G. Davies). London, SCM Press.

REVIEWS

1960 *A Book of Services and Prayers*, 1959, and *Congregational Anthem Book*, 1959 in *The Church Quarterly Review*, vol. CLXI, p. 388.

1961 A. Oakley, *The Orthodox Liturgy*, 1958 and N. Cabasilas (trs. J. Hussey and P. McNulty), *A Commentary on the Divine Liturgy*, 1960, W. S. Porter, *The Gallican Rite*, 1958 in *The Journal of Ecclesiastical History*, vol. XII, pp. 124–5.

E. C .Whitaker, *Documents of the Baptismal Liturgy*, 1960 in *The Journal of Ecclesiastical History*, vol. XII, p. 261.

N. M. Denis-Boulet, *The Christian Calendar*, 1960 and J. H. Dalmais, *The Eastern Liturgies*, 1960 in *The Church Quarterly Review*, vol. CLXII, pp. 376–7.

1963 C. E. Pocknee, *The Rite of Christian Initiation*, 1962 in *The Journal of Ecclesiastical History*, vol. XIV, p. 133.

P. Hammond, *Towards a Church Architecture*, 1962 in *C. R. Journal*, 1962, p. 28.

1964 J. G. Davies, *The Architectural Setting of Baptism*, 1962 in *The Journal of Theological Studies*, N.S. vol. XV, pt. 1, pp. 247–8.

1966 J. G. Davies, *Worship and Mission*, 1966 in *The London Quarterly and Holborn Review*, October 1966, pp. 328–9.

1967 M. P. Hubert, *Le Messe: Histoire du Culte Eucharistique en Occident*, 1965 in *The Journal of Ecclesiastical History*, vol. XVIII, p. 277.

The Taizé Daily Office (English trs.), 1966 in *The Church Quarterly Review*, vol. CLXVIII, pp. 521–2.

1969 W. Rordorf, *Sunday: The History of the Day of Rest and Worship in the earliest Centuries of the Christian Church*, 1968 in *The Journal of Ecclesiastical History*, vol. XX, pp. 315–6.

T. M. Finn, *The Liturgy of Baptism in the Baptismal Instruction of St John Chrysostom*, 1967 and C. E. Pocknee, *Water and Spirit*, 1967 in *The Journal of Ecclesiastical History*, vol. XX, pp. 320–1.

Bengt Sundkler, *Nathan Soderblom: his Life and Work*, 1968 in *Frontier*, May 1969, pp. 153–4

Gregory Dix (ed. H. Chadwick), *The Treatise on the Apostolic Tradition of St Hippolytus of Rome*, 1968 in *The Journal of Theological Studies*, N. S. vol. XX, pp. 629–30.

1971 R. W. Pfaff, *New Liturgical Feasts in Later Medieval England*, 1970 in *The Journal of Ecclesiastical History*, vol. XXII, pp. 265–6.

R. K. Pugh and J. F. A. Mason, *The Letter-Books of Samuel Wilberforce 1843–68*, 1970 in *The Journal of Ecclesiastical History*, vol. XXII, p. 375.

L. Sheppard (ed.), *The New Liturgy*, 1971 and E. C. Whitaker, *Documents of the Baptismal Liturgy*, 2nd edn 1970, in *The Expository Times*, vol. LXXXII, p. 189.

Peter J. Jagger, *Christian Initiation 1552–1699*, 1970, in *The Expository Times*, vol. LXXXII, pp. 249–50.

Horton Davies, *Worship and Theology in England: from Cranmer to Hooker, 1543–1603*, 1970 in *The Expository Times*, vol. LXXXIII, p. 57-8.

1972 R. J. Beckwith and J. E. Tiller, *The Service of Holy Communion and its Revision*, 1972, in *The Expository Times*, vol. LXXXIII, pp. 317–8.

D. M. Hope, *The Leonine Sacramentary, a Reassessment of its Nature and Purpose*, 1971, in *The Journal of Ecclesiastical History*, vol. XXIII, no. 4, pp. 370–1.

1974 J. G. Davies, *Everyday God: encountering the Holy in World and Worship*, 1973, in *The Heythrop Journal*, vol. XV, pp. 89–90.

J. D. Crichton, *Christian Celebration: the Sacraments*, 1973, in *The Heythrop Journal*, vol. XV, pp. 449–50.

1975 *Modern Ecumenical Documents on the Ministry*, 1975 and *A Critique of Eucharistic Agreement*, 1975 in *The Expository Times*, vol. LXXXVII, p. 59.

C. O. Buchanan, *Further Anglican Liturgies 1968–75*, 1975 in *The Expository Times*, vol. LXXXVII, p. 89.

J. D. Crichton, *The Ministry of Reconciliation*, 1974, and Kenneth Ross, *Hearing Confessions*, 1974 in *The Heythrop Journal*, vol. XVI, pp. 450–1.

J. H. McKenna, *Eucharist and the Spirit*, 1975 in *Alcuin Annual Report for 1975*, p. 2.

1977 R. F. Taft, *The Great Entrance: a History of the Transfer of the Gifts and other Pre-anaphoral Rites of the Liturgy of St John Chrysostom*, 1975 in *The Journal of Ecclesiastical History*, vol. 28, pp. 203–4.

A. H. Couratin and D. H. Tripp (eds), *Liturgical Studies by E. C. Ratcliff*, 1976 in *The Expository Times*, vol. LXXXVIII, p. 152.

1978 T. G. A. Baker, *Questioning Worship*, 1977 in *Theology*, vol. LXXXI, pp. 143–5.

G. Rowell, *The Liturgy of Christian Burial*, 1978 in *The Expository Times*, vol. LXXXIX, pp. 252–3.

1979 J. D. Crichton, *The Once and Future Liturgy*, 1977 and J. Gelineau, *The Liturgy Today and Tomorrow*, 1978 in *The Heythrop Journal*, vol. XX, pp. 89–91.

Cheslyn Jones *et al.*, *The Study of Liturgy*, 1978 in *The Journal of Ecclesiastical History*, vol. 30, pp. 295–6.

R. J. Beckwith and W. Stott, *This is the Day*, 1978, and S. Bacchiochi, *From Sabbath to Sunday*, 1977 in *The Journal of Ecclesiastical History*, vol. 30, pp. 475–6.

Cheslyn Jones *et al.*, *The Study of Liturgy*, 1978 in *The Expository Times*, vol. XC, p. 185.

George Every, *The Mass*, 1979 in *The Expository Times*, vol. XC, p. 215.

1981 J. D. Crichton *et al.*, *English Catholic Worship: Liturgical Renewal since 1900*, 1979 in *The Heythrop Journal*, vol. XXII, pp. 106–7.

Anon, *The Fear of Grace of the Lord*, 1980 in *The Expository Times*, vol. 93, pp. 189-90

1982 M. Perham, *The Communion of Saints*, 1980 in *The Heythrop Journal*, vol. XXIII, pp. 70–1.

R. Rutherford, *The Death of a Christian: the Rite of Funerals*, 1980 in *The Heythrop Journal*, vol. XXIII, pp. 227–8.

M. Hebblethwaite and K. Donovan, *The Theology of Penance*, 1981 in *The Heythrop Journal*, vol. XXIII, pp. 446–7.

M. J. Hatchett, *Commentary on the American Prayer Book*, 1980 in *Worship*, vol. 56, pp. 78–9.

Paul F. Bradshaw, *Daily Prayer in the Early Church*, 1981 in *The Expository Times*, vol. 93, p. 158.

1983 Paul F. Bradshaw, *Daily Prayer in the Earth Church*, 1981, in *The Heythrop Journal*, vol. XXIV, pp. 472–3.

1984 G. D. Kilpatrick, *The Eucharist in Bible and Liturgy*, 1984 in *The Expository Times*, vol. 95, p. 345.

1985 K. Stevenson (ed.), *Liturgy Reshaped*, 1982 in *The Heythrop Journal*, vol. XXVI, pp. 339–40.

G. J. Cuming, *A History of Anglican Liturgy*, 2nd edn 1982, in *The Heythrop Journal*, vol. XXVI, pp. 340–1.

K. Stevenson, *Nuptial Blessing: a Study of Christian Marriage Rites*, 1982 in *The Heythrop Journal*, vol. XXVI, pp. 341–2.

Y. Congar, *Diversity and Communion*, 1984, and D. Forrester and D. Murray (eds), *Studies in the History of Worship in Scotland*, 1984 in *The Expository Times*, vol. 96, pp. 154–5.

1987 J. Ratzinger, *The Feast of Faith: Approaches to a Theology of the Liturgy*, 1986 in *Theology*, vol. XC, pp. 309–10.

G. J .Cuming, *The Godly Order*, 1983 in *The Heythrop Journal*, vol. XXVIII, pp. 238–9.

G. W. Kilpatrick, *The Eucharist in Bible and Liturgy*, 1984 in *The Heythrop Journal*, vol. XXVIII, pp. 459–60.

A. Kavanagh, *On Liturgical Theology*, 1984 in *The Heythrop Journal*, vol. XXVIII, pp.462–3

K. W. Irwin, *Liturgy, Prayer and Spirituality*, 1984 in *The Heythrop Journal*, vol. XXVIII, p. 503.

1988 Michael Perham, *Liturgy, Pastoral and Parochial*, 1984 in *The Heythrop Journal*, vol. XXIX, p. 274.

1989 F. C. Senn (ed.), *New Eucharistic Prayers: an Ecumenical Study of their Development and Structure*, 1987 in *Worship*, vol. 63, pp. 86–7.

D. Forrester, J. I. H. McDonald and G. Tellini, *Encounter with God*, 1983 in *The Heythrop Journal*, vol. XXX, pp. 459–60.

1990 Michael Perham (ed.), *Towards Liturgy 2000*, 1989 in *Theology*, vol. XCIII, p. 165.

1991 George Guiver, *Company of Voices: Daily Prayer and the People of God*, 1988 in *The Heythrop Journal*, vol. XXXII, pp. 96–7.

J. D. Crichton, *The Living Christ: 'In Christ' through Scripture and Liturgy*, 1988 in *The Heythrop Journal*, vol. XXXII, pp. 267–8.

Bernard Botte, *From Silence to Participation: An Insider's View of Liturgical Renewal*, 1988 in *The Heythrop Journal*, vol. XXXII, pp. 429-430.

INDEX